A VIEW INTO ESSEX

A VIEW INTO ESSEX

by

Stan Jarvis

Foreword by Admiral Sir Andrew Lewis, K.C.B.
H.M. Lord Lieutenant of Essex

TERENCE DALTON LIMITED
LAVENHAM   .   SUFFOLK
1979

Published by
TERENCE DALTON LIMITED
ISBN 0 86138 053 3

First edition 1979
Revised edition 1986
Revised edition 1990

Text photoset in 10/11 pt. English

Printed in Great Britain at
The Lavenham Press Limited, Lavenham, Suffolk

Contents

This book is
dedicated to our children
Peter and Gwen
Robin and Susan

Index of Illustrations

Foreword

By Admiral Sir Andrew Lewis,
H.M. Lord Lieutenant of Essex

I AM very glad to have been given the chance to write a foreword to Stan Jarvis's latest, and most comprehensive, book on Essex; and he does not forget "Essex in London".

"History is the doings of people", he writes, and he devotes much of his book to telling us of the "doings" of many of the remarkable Essex men and women who have, over the centuries, from Saxon times to the present day, given to Essex its special flavour and appeal and made it the thriving county it is.

Born and brought up in Hampshire he has lived and worked in Essex for the last twenty years and brings to his task of telling us about this undervalued county all the enthusiasm of the convert. He is a man who loves his fellow men and wants to do his utmost to ensure that they will enjoy reading about, and be proud of, the county which many call home.

I recommend this book with confidence to all, whether they live in the county or not.

Andrew Lewis,
Finchingfield, September, 1979.

The Shire Hall, Chelmsford.

CHAPTER ONE

Essex—Where, When, What, Who

A POPULAR problem in our family quiz-games is to take a county and name all those which surround it. Essex is not such an easy subject as might be imagined. The fact that its southern limit is the Thames, with Kent across the estuary is a help, and the long, low irregular coastline to the east can easily be remembered. But as Essex represents the kingdom of the East Saxons it is hard to appreciate that Suffolk, the people of the south, lies north of it! Round the north and west, Cambridge and Hertfordshire spread, and, lower down, the River Lea once marked the boundary with Middlesex and London.

Today parts of old Essex have become the new Greater London Boroughs of Barking, Havering, Newham, Redbridge and Waltham Forest, which now hem the south and west of the county. The one and a quarter million people who live in these boroughs could be called Greater Londoners, but I believe they will continue to identify themselves with the old Essex which gave them the villages that can still be detected in the very heart of these conurbations. In their days of relaxation they will undoubtedly turn to the country near at hand for their rural pleasures and that is still Essex, all fifteen hundred square miles of it.

What is Essex made of? The answer lies in a brief study of its geology which influences the geography. One man at least has made himself a millionaire on the gravel which lies beneath the county's coat of clay. There are millions of tons of gravel, sand and cement being transported out of the county for building purposes, yet there is no stone at all in Essex. All the strata lie with a slope to the south-east, so that the lowest and therefore the oldest formations outcrop only in the north-west of the county, as can be seen in the chalk hills around Heydon and Langley—the dying fling, as it were, of the Chilterns. From there the surface soil changes through the later deposits of boulder-clay, sand, brick-earth and the gravel of the glacial drift and alluvial deposit to the almost all-pervasive London clay which gathers itself in humps, all under three hundred feet high, at High Beech, Danbury, Tiptree and Laindon.

Down in the south, between Purfleet and Grays, there is one remarkable exception to the general pattern. Here the chalk asserts itself at the surface—and suffers for it. Long before concrete became the all-purpose material it is today, chalk was being quarried to make whiting and Roman cement. Even before the Second World War, however, a staggering 400,000 tons of cement was being carried away by train and boat and lorry. The great chimneys of the cement works by the Dartford/Purfleet toll tunnel under the Thames gave smoky evidence day and night of vastly increased production until the recent recession in world trade.

1

The living and the dead: an Essex landscape.

The London clay sounds a very unromantic covering for most of the county. Yet it forms the cliffs from Harwich to Clacton as well as at Shoeburyness and Southend, and they cannot be said to be unattractive. In the area roughly between Colchester, Dunmow and Chelmsford it is often covered by the detritus of early glacier action.

The most exciting geological pointer to early life in our county is the outcrop of material called Red Crag, particularly where it forms part of the cliff at the Naze end of Walton-on-the-Naze. This formation is so rich in fossils of a Mediterranean-type climate that it is a veritable hunting-ground for the youthful amateur palaeontologist. One hundred and forty-eight species of mollusc have been found in fossil form here. A little display in the Chelmsford Museum of one day's collection includes the earbone of a whale and many fishes' teeth, all fossilised to the consistency of rock.

The overall geological structure makes for a gentle geography, a green and pleasant land. The ancient forests which once crowded in on the rivers have been hacked down by Saxon settlers who took advantage of the fertile soil which still today makes Essex a farming county, chiefly arable, though it is never a long walk to see a herd of cows or a flock of sheep. Essex is a great wheat-growing area; barley, too, is much in demand by maltsters, and sugar beet does well in the county where the first sugar factory in England was established at Ulting. Seed-growing is another local industry, the Sutton brothers started here in the Kelvedon area, and Essex rose growers are some of the most successful in the country. The county offers magnificent variety for walking and picnicking, and to the east, the expanse of marshland provides splendid isolation. Essex rivers, for the most part small and slow-moving, have their own personality.

The date of man's first appearance in Essex cannot even be guessed at. It is certain that there were men about when the county had no coast at all, but was joined to the continent, while the Thames and Rhine joined forces to flow northwards as one mighty river to the sea. The strata of loam, sand and gravel deposited by this old river system is most fruitful in evidence of early Essex settlers, for here more than anywhere else are found his stone implements. Great land changes have raised these gravel terraces above water level and their exploitation as a mineral source brought forth these discoveries. By now they have largely disappeared under the building expansion in areas like Leyton and Walthamstow, but the artifacts of the Stone Age still turn up in the valleys of the Roding and the Lea.

Cave-dwellers in other parts of the country have left evidence on the floors in the dark depths of their existence, but Essex had no such hiding places, only the fastness of the forest—so evidence of those ancient tribes is necessarily scant. One of the most curious relics must be the fossilised antler found at Little Thurrock and now in the British Museum. It has a mark which indicates a fracture during its life— a break which coincides with the form and fashion of one of those primitive flints wielded to good effect by early Essex man. Their weapons and implements developed, became more sophisticated, and when the technique of pottery was acquired, art quickly followed craft in the decoration of their daily utensils and in the design of their weaving on simple looms.

Their burial barrows, put up at such great pains, showed progression on another plane — man's respect for his own remains and a glimmer of his destiny in the order of nature. Those long barrows have disappeared, ploughed down to nothing in this agricultural county. Some evidence of a lake-dwelling community has come to light at Braintree to indicate an unusual variety of tribal settlement in Essex. The very abundance of neolithic weapons found at Walton-on-the-Naze could point to production on a "factory" scale, implying that trade over a considerable area had already begun.

The "Celtic" races who came to our shores after the great land divide brought with them across the Channel the knowledge of metal-working, or rather of the fusion of tin and copper to make bronze. This Bronze Age in Essex may be reckoned to have started twelve to fourteen hundred years B.C., continuing for at least seven hundred years. The clearest proof of the presence of these new people in our county is in the hoards of the smiths themselves. For example, the bronze-worker's hoard discovered at Hatfield Broad Oak included not only pieces of the copper and tin which were to be fused, but also the earthenware pots used in the process. That hoard can now be seen in the Colchester Museum. Similar finds from High Roding and Romford are in the British Museum and the Saffron Walden Museum respectively. The breadth of settlement at this time can be judged from the fact that hoards like this have also been found at Baddow, Danbury, Elmdon, Wendon, Fyfield, Thundersley and Grays. These câches of metal are memorials to those hardy, travelling smiths, marking the last place at which they worked on their roving commission. The products of their rough and ready workshops, bronze spears, daggers, swords and axes of beautiful design and finish, have been found throughout the county.

From about four hundred B.C. a new invading host crossed the sea, tribes who knew how to make harder implements and weapons of iron. But iron rusts, and after a couple of thousand years in the acid Essex clay there are not many items left to tell the story. Nevertheless, the boss of a shield and hand-made urn found as far apart as Wendon and Fambridge show the extensive nature of Iron Age settlements, and pottery of this period can be seen in every Essex museum.

It is from this Iron Age that earthworks, defensive or domestic, survive into our times. A classic example is Grym's Dyke, a three and a half mile-long rampart which was built about two thousand years ago, as a western defence for the great capital of *Camulodunum* (Colchester) where King Cymbeline ruled the tribes of eastern England. On the other side of the county is Loughton Camp in Epping Forest. Its choice as a vantage point is obvious. From the southern side it was possible to see clear across to the other side of the Thames. The strange Repell or Paille ditches at Saffron Walden date from this time, although the skeletons found on the site are from a later, Saxon cemetery. There are other examples of these Ancient British camps in the county, which will be dealt with in the appropriate chapters.

Their inhabitants were the people whom the Romans encountered when Julius Caesar came reconnoitring in 55 B.C. and they were the tribes who Emperor Claudius had to overcome in the successful invasion of 43 A.D. So complete was the victory that Roman colonisation continued on for four hundred years or more. Colchester has the honour of being the very first Roman colony established in this country, since the subjugation of King Cymbeline was one of the main aims in the invasion.

Roman roads were quickly pushed out all over the country. As the tribes settled more or less peaceably under Roman rule they gained much from the influence of that great civilisation. Places like Chelmsford began as Roman marching camps and ended as important tribal market centres. Chelmsford's Latin name, *Caesaromagues,* means Caesar's market, organised and administered with Roman efficiency and provided with temples, bath, theatres and of course, a market place with all the shops and trades a growing community required.

Great
Chesterford
in 1904.

*Essex Record
Office*

The mass of material provided by excavations from the eighteenth century onwards proves that the Roman presence in Essex was as extensive as it was intensive. Take Great Chesterford as an example. It is the merest village today, just off the A11 and right on the county's border, yet, apart from Colchester, it is the only Roman town in Essex known to have been walled. Through all its subsequent history the walls were being pulled down for the valuable building material of which they were constituted. Coins of the great King Cunobelin, or Cymbeline, issued under Roman licence were so plentiful that even in 1845 an archaeologist reported them as "universal all over the ground". Beside the living town there were no less than four cemeteries for the dead, which must in themselves be proof of peaceful occupation in large numbers over many years. Yet by 1945 a rush job had to be made of archaeological excavation because gravel workings threatened to destroy the whole site.

Roman Essex must have been an exciting place in which to live. Too exciting at times, for there was a fearful interlude when the Colchester tribe under Queen Boadicea rose in open revolt against their Roman overlords. As it was, the British were rid at last of their conquerors only because the Romans were urgently recalled to the defence of their homeland against the Gothic hordes at the beginning of the fifth century. As the legions disappeared the mixture of peoples left behind, called, for want of a better name, Romano-British, had to look after themselves.

Long before that the Romans had found it necessary to establish forts along the Essex coast to repel unwanted settlers. Without their presence the place became a prize for the tribes of northern Europe. Over a couple of centuries Essex was plundered and pillaged and ultimately taken over by the determined Saxons. That great and continuing work, the *Victoria County History* says, "Were it not for the unmistakable evidence offered by the county name it would be difficult to identify the founders of Essex with any particular branch of the Teutonic race that migrated westward as the Roman power declined." In other words, largely because they built in wood and wrought in iron, there are hardly any remains, archaeologically speaking, to tell their story.

They were firmly established here by 500 A.D., though it was not for another hundred years that they produced the first Anglo-Saxon coin, the sceatta, to replace the poor copies of Roman originals. It seems that the natural boundaries which outlined the county until very recent times were the original confines of the kingdom of the East Saxons. Most place-names as we know them today derive from the Saxons who came across the sea to carve their settlements out of the forests of Essex. There are so many places ending in "-ing"—the people of: "-ham"—the settlement of: "-don"—the hill of. Places like Canewdon, the Hill of Cana's people, and Ingatestone, people of the Great Stone, have changed their names subtly so that original meanings are hard to detect.

The first Saxon King of Essex was Sleda, followed by Sigebehrt, who died about 617. The last independent King was Sigered who by 823 was forced to bow to the King of Mercia. The men of Wessex finally took control however, by capturing Colchester in about 918.

The record would not be complete without a reference to the conversion to Christianity of the East Saxons. Though Mellitus was unsuccessful in his missionary endeavours in 604 the Saxon King Sigebehrt was eventually persuaded of the faith while on a visit to Northumberland. Subsequently he invited the priest Cedd to build a church in his land. That church, raised on the ruins of the old Roman fort at Bradwell around 650 is the subject still of an annual pilgrimage. Cedd was created Bishop of London and later made a Saint. Christianity altered the spirit of the people—and the face of the land, for now there would be three "skyscrapers" in every Saxon settlement, the hall for the assembly of the chief and his vassals, the mill to grind the corn—and the new church, raised high to the glory of God. To the inhabitants of the rude, mud hovels in the forest clearing these were skyscrapers indeed, on which they all had to work together at their chief's bidding.

That the Saxons were not left alone to enjoy their new-found Essex paradise is shown by the Viking remains which have come to light, and more particularly by that epic poem, "The Battle of Maldon"—one of the oldest literary relics in our language, of which Essex people justly can be proud. This poem recalls an eyewitness account of a great battle which took place between the Saxons and the raiding Danes on the mainland by the causeway to Northey Island in 991. The Danes had already burned down the great Abbey of Barking in 870, so it can be seen that the Saxons had much to contend with. By the eleventh century though, they were in total command, and a force to be reckoned with.

The death of King Edward the Confessor in 1066 brought the Norman invasion. The emphasis had passed from a local to a national "take-over" and so the Normans did not materially alter the life, the habits or customs of the Essex people. Essex had "jelled" under the Saxons and the life of the people persisted in the Saxon fashion. Essex, as we know it today, had arrived. Its history thereafter is part of the fabric of our national story.

CHAPTER TWO

Essex in London—and North-East to Margaretting

IT WAS the building of the first Bow Bridge early in the twelfth century and the raising of a causeway above the Stratford marsh which turned the main route from London to the eastern counties southward so that it strikes through the length of Newham. So the traveller who has crossed the River Lea by that famous bridge will start in the Essex of old at West Ham, now part of the new London Borough.

West Ham was remarkable for the density of its population more than a hundred years ago. First the London merchants made it their dormitory, then as the "wen" of London grew ever larger it became a factory area served by the Thames. "On its river bank have risen up the largest ship-building works in the world. Its quiet creek and marshland have been converted into mighty docks, furnishing a haven and a home for commerce from all countries of the earth." That is the view of a historian writing a hundred years ago.

Today the docks are doing less business, and the new system of containerisation is based on Tilbury docks. The humble dockers' dwellings have deteriorated and redevelopment has become a matter of concern for Newham. It was partly and grimly solved by the terrible bombing of the Second World War which laid waste much of the area. Since then the problem has been dealt with so energetically that the record of the last hundred years of West Ham can hardly be detected on the ground itself.

In Church Street, however, the old parish church of All Saints shows Norman work in its clerestory window arches, now blocked up, and on its walls there are fragments of those fifteenth century wall paintings which carried the message of the Bible to the illiterate. In those days the abbey of Stratford Langthorne, built in 1135, looked out across its open fields. Today its only visible remnant is a window frame of stone built into the long porch of All Saints. Yet for centuries it flourished on the proceeds of its property. It was landlord of East and West Ham put together and of parcels of land all over Essex. The religious order which owned it, the Cistercians, advocated good agricultural husbandry, so land was reclaimed and mills were built on the rivers. This was the origin of the famous Three Mills of Stratford, which became the home of Nicholson's gin distillery from 1730 until about 1968 when the firm was taken over by Bass, Charrington, Vintners Ltd. But the windmill went long ago, early in Victoria's reign, while the two tidemills, now known as House Mill and Clock Mill date from eighteenth and nineteenth century rebuildings. The owners have renovated the latter as a London business headquarters. There is every hope that the other will be restored as a local history branch of the Passmore Edwards Museum.

St. Andrew's Church, Greenstead-juxta-Ongar.

Newham can claim to have sheltered the first English calico printer, who set up his workshop by the River Lea in 1676. The Bow porcelain works, built on the north side of Stratford High Street around 1748, have made that bridge famous round the world. The factory closed about 1776.

After the bombing, the postwar development and the innovations to ease traffic congestion it becomes almost unbelievable that East Ham can boast of the only complete Norman church in the London postal area which was built as a parish church and continues so today. There is, hanging in the belfry still, a bell which was cast in 1381.

In Manor Park Cemetery, adjoining Wanstead Flats, there is a monument to a sixteen-year-old boy. Born in 1900 at Manor Park, he attended Walton Road School before becoming a boy in the Royal Navy. At the Battle of Jutland he stood by his gun, though badly injured, and his bravery earned him the posthumous award of the Victoria Cross. His old school was renamed after him the Cornwell Secondary Modern School and the children of East Ham collected for a monument to that gallant English boy, Jack Cornwell, V.C.

There are other people associated with Newham who have made significant contributions to national and even international progress. East and West Ham will always be remembered as the homes of Elizabeth Fry, the prison reformer, during thirty-six years of her life, and her brother Samuel Gurney, the banker, who owned what is now West Ham Park. The big obelisk in Stratford Broadway was erected to his memory. Elizabeth is buried in the Friends Burial Ground at Barking.

Another Quaker, Luke Howard, chemist and meteorologist, founded the Plaistow chemical firm in 1797 which still bears his name. He lived near it at Chesterton House. His monument is the system he invented for the classification of

8

clouds. It is still in use. Joseph Lister, born into a Quaker family in 1827 at Upton House, Upton, became the famous champion of antiseptic surgery. His name continues locally in the Lister Technical School at Plaistow.

The docks are much quieter these days. East India Docks bring to mind a vivid image of great sailing ships, the East Indiamen which came crowding up the Thames on every tide. Development of those docks down to our times is evident in their names, the Royal Victoria, the Royal Albert and the King George V docks. Their importance has been diminished by the continuing growth in the size of ships and by revolutionary methods of packing and handling. In the district round about there are names which are keys to Newham's early development. Beckton, for example, grew up around the great gasworks and is called after the governor of the company, S. A. Beck, and Silvertown was the result of the influence of the rubber works of H. A. Silver.

From the Beckton end of the borough it is a couple of miles up the High Street to the A118 which leads north east to Ilford, "the ford through the river Hyle"; that river is known today as the Roding. The place has lost its identity, submerged in the flood of building which makes it a dormitory for London. On the south side of Ilford Hill,

The Royal group of docks, photographed from the air in 1962.   *Port of London Authority*

along the High Road, stands the Chapel of St Mary and St Thomas of Canterbury. Part of this is the oldest building surviving in Ilford. Few realise its association with Barking Abbey. Adeliza, Abbess in the twelfth century, founded the hospital to house "thirteen lepers of the King's servants." It came to the crown upon the dissolution of that religious house and in 1572 Queen Elizabeth granted it to Thomas Fanshaw, a Remembrancer of the Exchequer. He still had to maintain the chapel and keep six poor, aged men. Services have continued at the chapel ever since.

In Valentines Park to the north is the oldest of the few mansions which have escaped development. In this case because it was purchased by the local authority for use as a housing office. It was built towards the end of the seventeenth century by James Chadwick, son-in-law of John Tillotson, Archbishop of Canterbury. The much venerated Hampton Court vine started life here as a cutting from the parent vine set in 1758, which an over-zealous gardener cut down in 1875.

The road goes on through Seven Kings, and here is a mystery. No-one knows how it received this name. The expert Dr Reaney in his *Place-Names of Essex* quotes the local tradition that seven Saxon kings came to a meeting here, but gives also the more prosaic interpretation of the Old English "Seofecingas" as "the settlement of the people of Seofeca".

Just north of Ilford is Barkingside where Dr Barnardo's "village home for destitute girls" was opened in 1873. Dr Thomas John Barnardo (1845 — 1905) was already known as a philanthropist when he founded the East End Mission for Destitute Children in 1867. In 1873 Mr John Sands, junior, another friend of poor orphans, gave him Mossford Lodge, Barkingside, on a rent-free lease for twenty-one years. He converted the rear part of the large house into a home for sixty girls, and by 1879, twenty-four "cottage homes" had been built in the 300 acres of grounds. At Barnardo's death in 1905 there were 64 cottages built and a total of 1,300 girls being cared for. Taken together with his Stepney home for boys it is reckoned that in his lifetime Dr Barnardo was directly responsible for the upbringing of a quarter of a million children. Today Mossford Lodge continues as a small part of the administrative centre of this wonderful institution which has expanded beyond even the dreams of the far-sighted founder.

As far out of London as Romford the London Boroughs lay claim to what was until very recently Essex territory, so Romford must now be part of Havering. Its one-way traffic system now circumvents the main shopping area and the market, too, can be enjoyed by pedestrians with less fear of accident. That market for all its noise and bustle is but a travesty of what it was down to the days after the Great War when Romford was a separate market town in its own right, drawing in crowds from its country districts and not a bit influenced by the doings of the great metropolis. Something of that atmosphere can still be enjoyed in the shadow of St Edward's church, while Romford takes on the new role of a shopping centre with car-parking facilities which make it more accessible than London's West End.

Havering includes Hornchurch and Upminster, two places with individual characteristics gained through growth over a thousand years. Hornchurch is so called because there is proof that from very early times horns were attached to the church as a form of decoration at the east end in place of the usual cross. The official guide sums up

10

the evolution of this settlement, " . . . in the short space of ten years to 1936, over 16,000 homes were built in Hornchurch and the population leaped by over 60,000 to 72,872."

St Andrew's church has a strong stone tower from which a copper covered spire rises to a height of 120 feet. The tower is thought to have been built at least six hundred years ago. Among the memorials a church of this age must gather is that to Thomas Witherings, "who originated the present day Post Office." He was appointed post-master for letters abroad in 1633 and quickly brought under efficient control what had become an unreliable service and crowned his achievements with the introduction of a registered letter service.

But Hornchurch will always be remembered for its recent history, the part its airfield played in two world wars. In 1916 the first three Zeppelins to be brought down over England were claimed by pilots from that airfield. Though it fell out of use for years it was rebuilt as an R.A.F. station in 1926 and during the Second World War it was the base from which the Spitfires fought in the Battle of Britain. Despite three concentrated attacks by German bombers on the aerodrome itself the Spitfires refused to be grounded. In the first year of the war they accounted for the destruction of 335 enemy aircraft with another 187 probably destroyed. In that time 73 British pilots did not return and 132 aircraft were lost. The station was closed in 1962, but the station badge is now in the proud possession of Havering Council.

A Hawker Hurricane of No. 71 Squadron prepares to take off, as so many did from the famous Battle of Britain airfield at Hornchurch during the hectic days of the summer of 1940.   *Gordon Kinsey*

Upminster, the frontier of London in Essex, gets its name from its situation on rising ground above the little Ingrebourne River. It is said to have been called Chafford in Saxon times, a contraction of St Chad's ford, for that worthy missionary is supposed to have operated from this centre in the seventh century. It is a pleasant residential place today, with easy access to rural Essex. The great landmark is a four-sailed smock mill of the late eighteenth century, unusually tall, now preserved by Havering Council.

In this great borough there is, on the south side of the chancel of Cranham church, a tablet to James Edward Oglethorpe, who was born in 1698, in London. As a Member of Parliament for thirty-two years he spent much of his time in the House trying to ease the lot of the prisoner, particularly in relation to the dreadful conditions in debtors' prisons. Seeing that colonisation might be an answer he led the expedition to Georgia in 1732 and organised the building of the settlement of Savannah. He signed a treaty with the Indians and brought back one of their chiefs to present him at court. An American has written of him, "He was the first Englishman who gave America its ideals of non-slavery and temperance." In the war with Spain in 1739 he was appointed General Officer Commanding British Forces in Georgia. He decisively beat the Spaniards, but used up most of his personal fortune in defending the colony. He returned to Britain in 1743 and married Miss Elizabeth Wright, of Essex. She brought to her marriage a very welcome fortune, which included Cranham Hall, right by the church, where they made their home. Through some intrigue he was brought to Court Martial and, though absolutely acquitted, it meant the end of his army career. He did not return to Georgia as he had intended but retired from public life to spend his married life as a country squire, until his death in July 1785. In 1925 Dr Samuel Jacobs of Oglethorpe University at Atlanta, Georgia received permission from the church authorities to open the family vault. He confirmed the presence there of the general's remains and a request to have them transferred across the Atlantic went to national levels before it was turned down. As a result there is a constant pilgrimage of Americans from Georgia to Cranham church to pay homage to the founder of their state.

From this edge of Havering it is necessary to return to the A12 if one wishes to follow in the path of the Romans to Brentwood. The wood about that place was brent, or burnt, to make a clearing for the settlement. It is hard to associate the present day town with that small patch of land won from the all-pervading forest to provide shelter for pilgrims on their way from all over East Anglia to the shrine of St Thomas à Becket at Canterbury. Pilgrims needed food and clothing too, so trade brought houses and shops, and Brentwood had begun.

The arts centre opened recently in Old House, a listed historic building, shows the progress of a thousand years of civilisation. Brentwood people can indulge in all kinds of artistic activities. The recital room was fitted out at the expense of the Ford of Britain Trust. This is understandable because the adminstrative headquarters of this great company are at Eagle Way, where Warley Barracks once stood. All that is left of that large range of military buildings is the chapel of the Essex Regiment, which had its base here until postwar amalgamation. The Regiment Museum which stood nearby has now been transferred to a wing of the Chelmsford and Essex Museum at Oaklands Park, Chelmsford.

Old House itself was once a boarding house of Brentwood School. It was in 1568 that the first school house was built, but Antony Browne, the successful lawyer knighted by Queen Elizabeth, had bought a piece of ground in October 1557 to fulfill the intentions of his will to provide "the Grammer School of Antony Browne, Serjeant at Law, in Brentwood".

Because Brentwood was at that time so small the folk still resorted to the parish church at South Weald, although the Abbot of St Osyth had built a chapel in the twelfth century, and its remains can still be seen in the High Street by the Odeon Cinema. To this day there is an annual pilgrimage of Brentwood schoolboys to the church where Sir Antony Browne was buried.

The one outstanding monument in the centre of Brentwood is the granite obelisk put up to the memory of William Hunter. Back in those days of religious intolerance this nineteen year old man caused a furore. He was a Protestant, and Queen Mary was aiming to restore Roman Catholicism. One day the vicar found him in the chapel, reading the Bible, for he had taught himself to read. The vicar fell into an argument with him concerning the nature of the Communion. The vicar was appalled at Hunter's views and reported him to the Lord of the Manor, that same Sir Antony Browne. He ordered the young man's arrest. Hunter had fled and his father was sent to search for him. He found him, but told him to flee while he went back and said he was unsuccessful. William thought his father would come to some harm in such a situation and so declared he would go back with his father to save him from punishment, and to stand by his faith.

Browne, in his questioning, could not shake that faith, so he sent him on to be examined by the Bishop of London as a heretic. Bishop Bonner promised him much if he would recant, even to employment in his own household. But William Hunter had declared his Protestant beliefs and stood by them. So on 26th March 1555 he was burned at the stake "at the town's end where the butts stood". Part of the original tree at which he was burned is still preserved in Brentwood School Museum. This tree originally stood in Ingrave Road opposite the Brentwood School Chapel.

The obelisk was raised at Wilson's corner on the side of the Shenfield Road in 1861 and rebuilt in 1910. The cracks now to be seen in the column were caused by the great heat of the fire of 1907, which destroyed the premises of Wilsons, then a drapers, now a departmental store, which still occupies the site.

In 1232 Henry III called to account Hubert de Burgh, the man who had been ruling the country during his minority. Hubert stopped at Brentwood on his way back to London to face the charges made against him. The king had sent three hundred soldiers there to arrest him, but he escaped into the sanctuary of the recently built chapel of St Thomas, holding the cross in one hand and the host in the other. The soldiers violated that holy sanctuary and dragged him off to London. However, when the news of the violation came to the ears of the Bishop of London he threatened the King with excommunication of all those implicated in the deed. But the King won and sent de Burgh back to that chapel at Brentwood under escort, then guarded the place so closely during the forty days grace which sanctuary offers that the virtual prisoner gave in and was once again taken to the Tower of London. It is nice to know that he was eventually allowed to keep part of his lands and live in retirement.

The William Hunter Memorial at Brentwood, cracked by the heat of a disastrous fire in 1907.

Less than a hundred years later, when Essex working men, with those of other counties, were seething under the repression of laws and taxes, Brentwood became the stage for acts of national importance. Essex men, called there to account for missing taxes, told the court on 30th May 1381 that they had already been told they need not pay this extra, iniquitous Poll Tax. It culminated in the great revolt and the first to die were some of the unfortunate jurors called to duty at that court. The incensed offenders caught three of them and beheaded them. The noise and bloodshed in the town must have been alarming and uncertainty reigned until the defeat of the peasants in a fierce battle at Billericay.

The church at South Weald has parts going back to 1150 and the strong tower was built in 1500. The beautiful alabaster reredos is lit most dramatically. It tells the story of the entombment of Jesus Christ.

Behind the church stood Weald Hall until its demolition in 1948. It was the home of the Tower family through two hundred years. Now the whole Park is open to the public. The parkland, with walks among the old gardens, round the lake and across its broad acres of greensward, makes an ideal picnic spot.

Shenfield, "fair, open country", is largely residential. The by-passing of Brentwood has brought some relief to this community whose church has much of interest. Inside there is a most unusual feature. The aisle has pillars and arches made most delicately in solid oak! The lack of stone in our county brought out the best in unknown fifteenth century craftsmen.

Mountnessing was for too long merely an irritating delay for drivers on the A12 but now it is bypassed and only those intent on visiting the village need leave the new highway. The local landmark is the three hundred year old post mill. Its warm red roundhouse, mellow-tiled, contrasts with the soaring white-painted, clapboard mill and its black, bonnet-like cap. Up to recent times there was of necessity a mill in every village in the county, but very few have survived as monuments to the miller's industry. This parish council very sensibly marked the celebration of the Jubilee of George V by restoring the mill, and village pride in its appearance continues, with the help of the County Council.

Almost opposite the mill on the other side of the road is the *Prince of Wales* which was originally the village bakehouse, so the corn was sown, grown, harvested, ground and baked virtually on the spot. In the bar one can see a list of tolls, done in cast iron, which was put up at the toll-gate on the great London Road. Without the money paid by travellers the local inhabitants could never have afforded to keep such a big and busy highway in repair.

Mountnessing church lies more than a mile to the southeast by the Hall, an inheritance from Saxon days. Its stout belfry, constructed entirely of huge beams in a complicated framework is a very typical Essex art. The west front and the chancel were built later, in the seventeenth and eighteenth centuries when the lack of stone was made up for by the production of bricks from local clay. A novelty in this remote country church is the fossilised rib bone of a mammoth or elephant found locally so long ago that it was venerated as being the remains of one of a race of giants who once inhabited the area.

The next village on, Ingatestone, also now requires a diversion from the fast main road. It is pleasant to walk the village street, appreciating the architecture, with only light local traffic to contend with. Its name gives the clue to the history of settlement here at the junction of two ancient trackways. At the crossroads by the church and on the other side of the road there are some boulders of "pudding stone" brought to Essex in the rolling action of glaciers in ages out of mind. They once were one great boulder, set up at that place to mark the parting of the ways. The Saxons called the settlers here the "ing" or people, at the Stone and so the name remains today. A much less romantic interpretation is that it was the Roman milestone on the great highway which the Saxons marked and made immortal.

Since the demolition of houses in front of the church it can be seen to good effect across a smooth green lawn which is a perfect foil for the red Tudor brickwork. The fine fifteenth century tower is decorated with a diaper pattern of black bricks. The connection with the local ruling family is evinced in the number of monuments to Petres all down the years. They include the tomb of Sir William Petre, founder of the great and continuing Essex family, who died in 1572.

He was originally from Devon, but had come to London as Secretary of State and confidant of kings. In 1538 he leased the Manor of Ingatestone from the Abbess of

Barking, so that he was able to buy the land from the King when the Abbey was suppressed. On it he built Ingatestone Hall, which stands, and is still lived in by the family.

Nearby Fryerning has Roman brick in the building, and it has quietly carried on as a settlement from that date. In the vestry can be seen an unusual memento of early worship, a palimpsest, or memorial brass which has been engraved on both sides. One side records a fifteenth century burial and the other perpetuates the memory of one Mary Gedge, a century later. Green Street and Mill Green lie further in the Essex greenery, where another crippled windmill stands, and the local inn, the *Viper,* claims to be the only one of this name in the country.

Margaretting is just another village when seen from the passing car, but its individuality is expressed in two widely separated parts of the parish. At Margaretting Tye on the lane to Stock there is a prehistoric tumulus used by an enterprising millwright as a mound for a windmill. Much further down the old road to Ingatestone there is the turning to Margaretting Hall and the church, now separated by the railway. Choose a day when the sunshine is flooding through the east window of St Margaret's, the church that gave the place its name, and you will see the glowing colours of the fifteenth century Flemish glass which depicts the Tree of Jesse, representing the genealogy of Jesus Christ from the "root of Jesse". The shingled spire and belfry are supported by a massive arrangement of beams which appear to be as sound as when they were first trimmed with the adze five hundred years ago.

The gatehouse at Ingatestone Hall.

Owen Keen

16

CHAPTER THREE

County Town and All Around

CHELMSFORD, viewed from any approach road, is unprepossessing. In the flat lands of the river plain it is hardly noticeable. Only the modern multi-storey developments catch the eye from the busy A12 road which, opened as a bypass in 1933, is now the most dangerous street in town. However, a new, widely-diverging by-pass is planned to pass well to the south.

Then the people on the new estates which now merge imperceptibly with the old village of Great Baddow will be able to move and breathe more freely. They will be able to travel easily into the centre of the county town where a multi-storey car park caters to the users of the pedestrian precinct.

There is a better face to Chelmsford despite the fact that so many of the buildings with historical associations have been torn down. A typical walk through history could start by the Borough Council offices in Duke Street above the railway station. In the area library, once part of this civic centre, but now in an extension of County Hall, there is an Essex Collection which is crammed with books on the county in general and Chelmsford in particular. One could learn the whole history and character of the town without stirring from this wonderful library.

The walk to the High Street and the town centre outlines the changing role of Chelmsford in a modern prosperous county. Little shops and small town houses of Georgian and Victorian character have been converted into or replaced by the rather tawdry embellishments of a score of building society offices.

On the right hand side behind the offices of solicitors and estate agents rises the mighty new block of County Council offices. The 1935 offices down the street, more permanently appointed, are worth a visit to see, on the second floor, the wall paintings and stained glass planned as an entity by Vincent Harris, R.A. and given to the county by Mr William Julien Courtauld of the famous spinning and weaving family.

In the lobby of the main entrance are two stained glass windows, each of twelve lights, with designs by Kruger Gray of the coats-of-arms of Essex abbeys and priories on the left and of the founders of ancient Essex schools on the right. The murals in the lobby show, on the one hand, Queen Elizabeth I addressing troops at Tilbury on the approach of the Spanish armada, by A. K. Lawrence, R.A., and on the other of Queen Victoria dedicating Epping Forest to the use of the public in 1882, by Melville Lewis.

The Council chamber windows include a further series of Essex coats-of-arms and murals which show scenes from Essex history, portraits of Essex people of note and two maps which show the county in the sixteenth century and recent times.

The former Library, Chelmsford, with the Civic Centre behind.

Very soon after this 1935 County Hall is passed Duke Street gives on to Tindal Square, where several of Chelmsford's connections with the past can be studied. The statue in the middle of this is of Sir Nicholas Conyngham Tindal. Of all the men and women who helped to administer the past and fashion the future of our county town the only one to have a statue erected to his memory is Tindal. A few years ago he was lifted bodily, plinth and all, and dumped down unceremoniously a few yards further back from the Shire Hall in order to improve traffic conditions. Tindal was a young man of fourteen when the Shire Hall was being built. He was born on 12th December 1776 at Coval Hall in Moulsham Street, where the florist's is today. On the side of the shop there is a plaque marking the site. He was the son of Robert Tindal, a well known Chelmsford solicitor and great grandson of Nicholas Tindal, historian.

Young Nicholas went to the local grammar school, built in 1629 where the 1935 part of County Hall stands today. On the way to school he would have stopped to watch the building of the old stone bridge, for it was finished in 1787, when he was a lad of ten. What excitement it must have given the daily journey from Moulsham to Chelmsford to see the river that divided them diverted while the workmen built the big new buttresses. That was not the only diversion to make him late home when

Old houses bordering the Cathedral yard, Chelmsford. ▶

school was out. The old Sessions House in the middle of Tindal Square as we know it today was falling into a ruin and so the Shire Hall had been slowly building behind a veritable forest of scaffolding and ladders. I wonder, when he saw the workmen installing those three plaques high up on its face, representing wisdom, justice and mercy, whether he remotely dreamt that his future lay in just such a court of law.

At nineteen he went on to Trinity College, Cambridge and in 1801 he was elected M.A. and became a law student the following year. His father may have intended him to follow in the family practice, but Nicholas Tindal soared above that. After being called to the Bar in 1809 he joined the Northern Circuit. In 1824 he entered Parliament and within two years he was appointed Solicitor-General and also received a knighthood. Finally he was appointed Chief Justice of the Court of Common Pleas on 9th June 1829 and continued in this office judging cases to within ten days of his death in 1846.

As for the Shire Hall itself, the interior has been changed to suit modern administration but the county room, a great ballroom upstairs, preserves its richly elaborate ceiling and frieze, and the Picture Room has canvases of unequal artistic value but of interesting local significance.

Behind the Shire Hall, with access from Duke Street or New Street on either side, is the parish church of St Mary's, which was elevated to the status of Cathedral in 1914. It is highly possible that a Saxon church was reared on this site, but the earliest evidence of a holy building here is some stones in the tower which show traces of Norman work. Generally the building dates from an extensive fifteenth century restoration, though this church is, of course, the ever-changing outward sign of the spiritual enthusiasm of generations of worshippers. For example, the beautiful Perpendicular south porch has in its upper storey the library presented to the parish in 1679 by Dr Knightbridge. That same porch was restored and embellished in 1953 to stand as a memorial to American airmen stationed in Essex during the Second World War.

The tower is about ninety feet high and houses a peal of thirteen bells. Within the Cathedral there are a number of interesting details, from the big cupboards built into the pillars to take the props and costumes of the early church plays for which Chelmsford was famous in the county, to the other pillars, made of an early concrete called Coade stone, to replace the damage caused when the church fell down in 1800.

From the steps of the Shire Hall the view down the High Street has considerably changed since those days of the sixteenth and seventeenth centuries when the witches were sentenced to death in the Sessions House on this spot. On the right the buildings on one side of Tindal Street, including a couple of ancient inns, have been totally demolished in the completion of the pedestrian precinct.

On the left the *Saracen's Head* retains its old face, reminder of the days when Anthony Trollope could have been seen inside. It is said that he actually wrote some parts of his novels there. Just a little further on, on the same side, is the pleasing brick frontage of the Mansion House, or Judge's Lodging. Its name proclaims its early use. At the foot of the High Street that old stone bridge still stands the weight of modern traffic; a flow never anticipated by its designer, John Johnson, the same man who, as County Surveyor, was responsible for the design and erection of the Shire Hall in 1791. Strange to think that in the days of the plague a sentry was placed on the bridge to prevent Moulsham people bringing their dead for burial in the churchyard, in case they should bring infection to the town and ruin trade!

Moulsham Street is probably the best preserved street of old houses in the town, yet many houses and shops have been demolished, to make room for the inner ring road, or to be replaced by modern buildings which have in most cases been specially designed to harmonise with the street scene. Here the smaller shops survive and the air of the old market town lingers on. Way up this street, just before its junction with New London Road, there is, on the left, Oaklands Park, one of the prettiest places in town.

More important to the tourist is the fact that "Oaklands", the house itself, is the Chelmsford and Essex Museum. The history, people and places of our county are no more clearly evidenced than in the collections on view daily. One large room and a small gallery are given over to constantly changing exhibitions from all over Britain, and on a variety of themes.

From New Street by the Shire Hall it is possible to get to the leisure centre, which includes swimming pools and sports halls which attract thousands of enthusiasts down the appropriately named Waterloo Lane. Across the car park is Springfield Mill—that village once extended in this direction. The mill has done duty as a licensed restaurant in recent years.

It was in the mellow brick Georgian miller's house, which contrasts with the white, wooden bulk of the mill, that Joseph Strutt was born on 27th October 1749. His father Thomas, the miller, was already a wealthy man who had married Elizabeth Ingold, daughter of the miller at Woodham Walter. But he died within a year of Joseph's birth and Elizabeth had to bring him up and his older brother John, who became a famous London doctor, on her own. Joseph showed some artistic talent, so he was apprenticed to the engraver, W. W. Ryland. When he was twenty he enrolled at the Royal Academy. In less than a year he had gained one of the first Silver Medals awarded, and the following year carried off a gold medal for his skilful work.

Then he was introduced to the great reading room of the British Museum and found there a storehouse of information on the ancient customs of our country which was to occupy his interest and his labours through most of his life. His wonderful skill in drawing and engraving became the servant of his antiquarian interest and the series of books which resulted are valued today not only for their historical integrity, but also for the beauty of their production. There can be very few authors of all time who were able to draw and then engrave the illustrations to their own writings. That is what makes Joseph Strutt rather special.

His first book, *The Regal and Ecclesiastical Antiquities of England* was published in 1773. Its success set the pattern for further books, each painstakingly researched. It took three years to prepare the next volume, *Manners, Customs, Arms, Habits, Etc. of the People of England* which was, again, fully illustrated. By 1778 he finished his *Chronicle of England*. He was still living in Chelmsford, although his research took him to London so much that he bought a house there as a matter of convenience soon after his marriage in 1774. On the death of his wife four years later Strutt gave up research for seven whole years and turned to painting for solace. He had nine of his paintings exhibited at the Royal Academy.

He started again with the two-volume *Biographical Dictionary of Engravers*, which was so detailed that it has remained the basis of subsequent compilations on this subject. Despite further personal difficulties Strutt continued writing and illustrating. Following three volumes on the *Dresses and Habits of the English People* which was completed by 1799, he brought out *Sports and Pastimes of the People of England* in 1801, which is his best known work today and has very recently been reprinted.

The very last work which the fifty-two-year-old miller's son embarked upon was a novel, an historical romance called *Queenhoe Hall,* but he died on 16th October 1802. It was left to Sir Walter Scott to finish the book with a last chapter and bring it out under his own name. Joseph was buried in the churchyard at Holborn. That old mill and the house in which he grew up still stand across the Chelmer. The mill is slowly falling apart from lack of use and maintenance. When it does eventually fall down and is bulldozed away it will mean breaking yet another of the few remaining threads the town still has with its past, therefore it must be preserved.

But at least there is one more modern building which will be preserved. The old silk factory in Hall Street bears proudly the second of the only two commemorative plaques put up in Chelmsford, for it was used by the famous Marconi to set up the very first radio factory in the world in 1898.

We should not leave Chelmsford without reference to a man who has appeared in no history book on Essex so far, although without him there would not be preserved a vast collection of Essex people and places as they looked on both sides of the twentieth century. Frederick Spalding was born in 1858 and died in 1947. It is thanks to that man and his father that many reminders of old Chelmsford have been preserved to future generations, in the form of hundreds of photographs of the town and of villages for miles around. Many of them have Spalding's own comments written on the mounts in further identification. It all began with Spalding's father who set up business in Tindal Square, as a self-taught photographer in the earliest days of the new art.

21

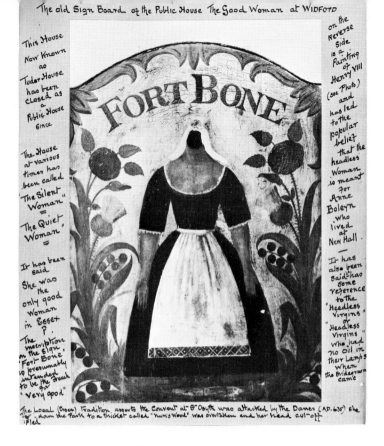

The old Sign Board of the Public House The Good Woman at WIDFORD

This House Now Known as Tudor House has been closed as a Public House Since

The House at various times has been called "The Silent Woman" = "The Quiet Woman" =

It has been said She was the only good Woman in Essex?.

The inscription on the sign "Fort Bone" is presumably intended to be the French "Très good" or "Very good"

on the Reverse side is a Painting of Henry VIII (see Photo) and has led to the popular belief that the headless Woman is meant for Anne Boleyn who lived at New Hall.

It has also been said it has some reference to the "Headless Virgins" or "Headless Virgins" who had no oil in their Lamps when the Bridegroom came

The Local (Essex) Tradition asserts the Convent at S.t Osyth was attacked by the Danes (A.D. 635) she, down the Path to a Thicket called "Nun's Wood" was overtaken and her head cut off fled

One of Fred Spalding's photographs: the writing is in his own hand.

Young Frederick grew up in the house above the business and was made a councillor in 1891, only three years after the incorporation of the town as a borough, and continued for fifty-four years. He was elected an Alderman in 1913 and then chosen as Mayor for three consecutive years from 1922. On 25th October, 1933, in his seventy-fifth year, he was made an Honorary Freeman of the Borough as a public appreciation of his service to the town. When he completed fifty years service with the Council in 1945, a resolution of congratulation and appreciation was passed with acclamation.

In the District Library there are now kept the old stock books of the picture postcards which Fred Spalding photographed, processed, multiplied and sold. They show villages and views all around Chelmsford and far beyond and represented years of hard work. Just as fascinating in their volume and variety are the photographs of Chelmsford taken by father and son which take the story of the town from the eighteen seventies through to the nineteen thirties. He was glad to talk about the town at meetings of various societies. His ancient brass lantern with a collection of hundreds of glass slides was still in use up to five years ago, for members of the library staff gave talks based on his material.

Fred Spalding is still loved and respected by anyone who looks through the enormous collection of photographs in the public library and the Essex Record Office which demonstrate his love for the town and the county, and also his consummate skill as a professional photographer.

22

St Mary's, Widford.

Owen Keen

In its expansion over the years the county town has swallowed some of the old villages which once were a mile or more away down country lanes. Widford to the south west on the A12 has quite lost its identity. *The White Horse* inn has changed considerably from the photograph taken by Fred Spalding in 1887, but its basic construction can still be traced in the modern building which, within, offers all the comfort and convenience of our age.

There once stood, on the other side of the road, an inn with the most unusual sign. It was called *The Silent Woman*, and the signboard, now preserved in the Chelmsford and Essex Museum, portrays a woman with her head cut off. The original name of the inn was the *Good Woman*, and this may well refer to none other than St Osyth whose name is well known in the county for her Christian martyrdom at the hands of the Danes back in the seventh century. Yet the signboard now preserved shows on its reverse a portrait of Henry VIII, because local tradition had it that the lady who is shown headless is none other than one of his ill-fated wives, Anne Boleyn, who lived at one time at New Hall, Boreham.

The church of St Mary was built in 1862 at the sole cost of Arthur Pryor, owner of the great Hylands mansion which is now the property of the townspeople of Chelmsford. The property includes a park of some four hundred acres which has been preserved in its natural state. The very naturalness of this park, the fact that there are no amenities for sports and games, no kiosks for refreshment, is the very reason for its popularity.

Vacillation by the town and district councils over the entire period of their ownership has doomed the mansion as repair costs soared year by year. It is now a ruin, literally falling down, and cost of restoration is apparently beyond public funds. It was built about 1728 for Sir John Comyns, chief Baron of the Exchequer and the family lived there until 1797 when it was sold to Cornelius Kortwright. He it was who commissioned William Atkinson, between 1819 and 1825, to design the great portico of Ionic columns we see today. The grand interior will never be seen again, for the place is in such a dangerous condition that no-one is allowed to enter.

The last owners, the Hanburys, husband, wife and the only son who was killed in a flying accident in the last war, are buried in a little consecrated area of the gardens they once so enjoyed. In those days entrance to the estate was off the A12 at Widford; the entrance today is via the village of Writtle.

There is a connection between Widford and the scattered settlement of Galleywood which has never been sufficiently nucleated to be called a village.

Legend has it that two brothers owned neighbouring estates. They fell out over the ownership of the church pew. The man at Widford had the church pulled down and put up the present structure with a tall steeple. Whereupon his brother erected on his land at Galleywood a church of exactly the same dimensions which was taller than Widford's—because it was on higher ground.

In fact the two churches were built at the expense of that Arthur Pryor already mentioned. The one at Galleywood, dedicated to St Michael and All Angels was erected in 1873. This church has the unusual reputation of being the only one in the country built inside a race track. Galleywood Common was the site of the Chelmsford race course for more than a hundred years, until it was sold prior to the last war. The course itself can still be clearly detected.

The church at Chignall St James.

In the solution of the housing problems of an ever-increasing population Galleywood and Great Baddow merge imperceptibly into the urban landscape of Chelmsford, but Great Baddow is very much a village still and the building of the bypass in recent years has preserved its atmosphere. The modern is represented by the flats which tower above the shopping precinct on the site of the old Vineyards estate. The ancient is just as evident, in the grand old church of St Mary's which, through tremendous local effort, has recently been restored. The beautifully kept churchyard is a green carpet dotted with white stones, against which the grey flint of the tower, interspersed with Roman tiles, and the Tudor brick work of the battlemented nave and porch stand out with strikingly beautiful effect.

In late Saxon times Great Baddow was just part of the well-ordered estates of Algar, Earl of Mercia. He was succeeded by his son Eadwine who, when the Normans came, refused to support King Harold. When Harold was slain he tried unsuccessfully to gain support from the citizens of London to be declared their sovereign. Next he submitted to the Conqueror on condition that William should give him his sister in marriage. William accepted the submission and promised the marriage, but when safely on the throne rejected Eadwine. Eadwine tried to raise a rebellion, and was slain, so the king took over all his lands and vested them in the monastery of the Holy Trinity at Caen.

Through the wisdom of latterday planning the village of Writtle to the west of Chelmsford preserves its identity. So today Writtle still retains its character as a village. The large estates built round it must have brought a burden on the local services, but they have given homes to hundreds, and the village centre stands serene; its pond and greens, its houses and shops telling, in their varied and interesting facades, the story of the place down the ages.

In the Church of All Saints memorials of engraved brass on very early tombs bring brass rubbers from far and near. Such activity is a mixed blessing, as one student, evading the proper fee for making a rubbing, made endless copies of one particularly good Writtle brass and sold them at a high price in London. He was really subsidised by the parishioners who regularly contribute to the upkeep of the church.

It is beautifully kept—and beautiful is hardly good enough to describe its appearance during the recent flower festivals. With its ancient memorials, its records of village folk going back to 1634, and with its stout walls and sturdy tower it looks set to last for ever. But that very tower dates only from 1802. One stormy night in that year one wall of the tower fell away completely, leaving the bells swinging in the gale. Within a day the whole tower, bells and all came crashing to the ground.

A whirlwind storm in October 1916 took the roof off the *Cock and Bell*. Colin and Zena Henton, the present landlords, have commissioned a pamphlet which tells the history of this inn from the eighteenth century.

The Rose and Crown is at the top of the hill and on the right is St John's Green, with old houses dotted about, one or two even now being renovated to make homes for hopeful young newly-weds. The Marconi works behind that old-world vista of timber and plaster houses overlooked by oak and elm, from which the first public entertainment broadcast in the world was made in 1922, have been closed down. The dead village heroes of two world wars are commemorated with a simple cross under the trees below the pond, a home for an interesting variety of water birds.

Almost any day in the holidays you will find a knot of optimistic young fishermen down by the bridge over the Wid, which in its old form of Writtolaburna, gave the village its name. It means "the babbling, purling stream." Perhaps it was just that, even down to the time, in 1211, when King John had his hunting lodge built, where the Institute of Agriculture stands today down Lordship Lane, so that he might hunt in the extensive forest which was Essex. Today, though, the poor old river, drained and diverted against flooding, exploited as a supply of water, used as a dump for old prams and the like has a pretty hard time of it.

Writtle is by far the largest parish in Essex reaching far from its village centre across the A414 and right up to the Chignall villages. Once there were three of these centred on the churches of St James, St Nicholas and St Mary. But St Mary's church vanished time out of mind and Chignall St James and Chignall Smealey remain the two separate villages.

Chignall St James is such a small place and the church was plain and humble. It has been declared redundant, sold and converted into a house of much-sought-after character. The stone that marks the grave of Miller Christy is hardly recognisable in the small churchyard. He was born in 1861 and died in 1928. Any library on Essex would be scattered throughout with his writings. From his boyhood spent at the Quaker School at Epping he was interested and active in studying natural history. When he was twenty-nine he went to Canada as a member of the Tuke Emigration Commission which aimed to settle Irishmen in Manitoba and his observations of the natural history of that place were published, in 1885, as *Manitoba Described*. From this beginning a long list of books and periodical articles flowed, the majority of them on his own well loved county of Essex. Not least among them was the *Handbook of Essex* published in 1887 which covered the history of every town and village in the county in the most comprehensive fashion. His versatility is further shown in his *Trade Signs of Essex* published in the same year and in the very full section on trades and industries of Essex which he wrote for that great and continuing work, the *Victoria History of the County of Essex*.

His natural curiosity led him to abstruse investigations like those on the audibility in Essex of the gunfire on the Western Front during the First World War. He was also one of the founders of the Essex Field Club. Yet now, despite an active life in the public eye he lies quite forgotten and unremarked.

The Tudor church at Chignall Smealey is a mellow reminder in warm red brick of the essential part this place of worship played as the very heart of the community.

When I visited it one spring weekday the primroses were out along the banks beside the road. The church was deserted but for the priest who was conducting morning service, without music. I sat in a pew as his whole congregation. "I know no-one has come to church," he said, " but as they work for my and our benefit in the fields and factories I feel it my duty to intercede with God on their behalf as regularly as they go to work." A moving sentiment and a meeting which cannot be done justice to in cold print.

From the Chignalls it is but a degree round the compass to Broomfield. Go out along the Broomfield Road today and it is hard to tell where the town ends and the village begins. It derives its name from the broom which thrived on its gravelly soil, and was fashioned by the villagers into brooms to sweep the cottage floors when hard-beaten Essex clay was the universal carpet.

It was summed up, long before my grandfather's time as, "fruitful in its soil, convenient, pleasant and healthy in its situation." And it was just these qualities which down the years made the charming village a dormitory of the county town. But the village is still there, if you care to look for it. True, as you leave Chelmsford you see the hand of development heavy on the parish. Broomfield Lodge has gone, and many other big, old residences of an earlier generation of Chelmsford businessmen and city fathers have been taken over by a variety of organisations, including the County Council and Marconis. Without servants, without modern conveniences, or central heating, the gracious living of those large houses became a nightmare existence, so their passing should not be mourned. Many of them have been demolished so that better use may be made of their land for urgent housing needs.

Thus Woodhall is now a council housing estate, but once it was the Hall of no less a person than the well-known Lord Rich.* Patching Hall, off the lane named after it, has been replaced by modern flats. That is rough justice on the old place really, because the barns there were built of an even earlier demolition of part of the vast New Hall at Boreham. From here the lane runs on up past the St. John Payne School with a right turn where modern houses with neat gardens line the road.

There is a human story inside every one of these houses, but at one an ambulance stands by in the garage every day. Every night, the lady who lives there must go to hospital if she is to awaken to a new dawn. Miss Elizabeth Twistington Higgins moved here from Kent some years ago, but she needed help, for she is almost totally paralysed. She can only move her head and, because those muscles by which we breathe through reflex action are paralysed, she must remember to breathe. Every breath is a conscious effort and because she cannot make that effort when she is asleep, Miss Twistington Higgins must rely on an artificial lung at Broomfield Hospital every night of her life.

What an example she is to us active people who moan about an attack of 'flu or complain of aching feet. But she does not leave it at that. She reads by using a

* See also Chapter Nine

page-turner held in her mouth, she telephones by blowing into a special instrument, she paints beautiful pictures with brushes held between her teeth, she has given radio and television interviews and she gets out and about. One series of trips is to rehearsals of the Chelmsford Ballet Company to give informal advice, much valued because before she was paralysed she was an accomplished dancer and instructor in her own right. Her recently published biography, *Still Life*, is another tribute to her indomitable will.

From this story of a modern Broomfield inhabitant it is not far up the same road towards the Chignalls, and Priors, which stands on the left and is so called because it once belonged to the Priors of Blackmore. A century ago it remained uninhabited for years because of a strong local rumour that it was haunted.

A hundred and fifty years ago the population consisted of 321 male and 303 females. Today that number of people is accounted for in just one of the many estates all around the village centre. But for anybody interested there is still the nucleus of the village around School Lane and by the church.

Before I tell you about the church I should say that a recent vicar, the Reverend A. J. Caton, was not only well known in his parish, he achieved a reputation which spread from Britain across the Atlantic to the United States—as the author of Western stories! It is great credit to the incumbent of a quiet English parish that he could write such stories so authentically that they were bought even by the people living in the area of which he wrote.

The church of St Mary was constructed in faith, restored with reverence and mellowed by time. It was damaged by bomb blast in the Second World War, but who could believe that today? The walls show how the Norman Christians made the best use of material immediately to hand. They picked up all the Roman bricks and tile still lying about five hundred years after the legions had left for their homeland, and they added all the flint they could find in the gravelly clay and finally they kept a sharp eye for pieces of "pudding stone". This strange natural conglomerate of rock and gravel looks very much like large lumps of a modern, rough concrete mix, when turned up under the plough. The present nave and chancel were built of these materials soon after the Norman conquest.

The tower was built in the twelfth century, one of only six round towers in Essex, and there are many theories about these towers. I like the one that holds that the church was the only substantial building in the village and the circular tower could command a view all round, so that when the wild men from the north came marauding across the seas to raid far inland the church could be fortified: the slits in the tower made good firing positions for bows and spears and the villagers could all crowd in together till the trouble was past.

The door shows, inside, the round Norman arch which proves its ancestry. A number of brasses and the square, carved stone font take the story on down the ages. In this century a restoration of the church brought to light a niche which had been plastered over. In it had been placed a Bible which once belonged to Charles I. Its story is revealed in a note on the inside cover, "This Bible was King Charles the First's, afterwards was my grandfather's, Patrick Younge, Esq., who was Library Keeper to his Majesty, now given to the Church at Broomfield by me, Sarah Atwood, Aug ye 4th, 1723."

Broomfield church in 1973.

So it was already about eighty years old when the church received it. Younge was himself buried in the chancel under a slab of black marble which has been so worn by the feet of communicants that it is now almost unreadable. It states that one of his daughters was married to a John Atwood. He lived in the old Parsonage House, now but a slight bump in the gardens of the present building.

The clue to the Bible's vicissitudes is in a letter from a Colonel Lucas of Witham to the Reverend W. Trimmer, then Vicar, after he had visited his old haunts in October 1892. "...I was glad to see the old font replaced. It was my good fortune to rescue it from being sold as old stone. It was for years sunk in your stable yard as a drinking trough for horses . . . I also saved King Charles's Bible, which I suppose you have. That was in a dirty old brown paper cover lying on the floor with a lot of a dozen or so old books, and had I not happened to pick it up and feel the embossed cover through the paper, it, too, would have been sold in some lot of 'one dozen vols., various,' for 1/- or 1/6!" When Cromwell declared the Commonwealth, and churches were defiled through mistaken Puritan zeal, some person carefully hid that Bible so that it should be preserved to a future generation and, in God's own time, that Bible was discovered and is now the church's principal treasure.

Thank goodness the churchmen of today are conscious of the need to preserve such interesting items of village history. The interest of the congregation and the villagers at large in Broomfield's past has been stimulated by the annual issue since 1974 of a booklet compiled by a Group of the Broomfield Parish Council. The glimpses it offers of village life, ancient and modern are as fascinating as they are diverse. The interest, for example, in the preservation of Wollards Cottages, on Church Green, once threatened with demolition, brought a complete account of their origin as two tenements given "to the use of the Poor of Broomfield forever" by the will of Thomas Woollard on 20th February 1700.

The church has had another illustrious vicar in the person of Philip Morant, the great Essex historian whose book in two elephant folio volumes published around 1776 is today as scarce as it is interesting. He was here for five years and has so much to say in his great history about his old parish that it cannot all be quoted here, but any Bromfield (as he spells it) inhabitant can read the full account in the public library, and enjoy the quaint phraseology of an earlier age. For example:

"1. The Maner of Bromfield Hall.
The mansion-house stands near the church. At the time of the survey (Domesday) it was in Goisfrid de Magnavilla, or Geffrey de Mandeville, who came into England with William the Conqueror; and was rewarded by him with a hundred and eighteen Lordships, whereof forty in Essex, and this among the rest . . . "

Then he traces the ownership of the Hall all the way down to the seventeen seventies when "John Olmius, Esq" inherited it.

Ruth, the widow of William Marriage of Partridge Green Farm, way up beyond the hospital, died on 11th March 1772 and asked to be buried in her own orchard as she was a Quaker. Her wish was complied with and her tomb has been reverently restored and preserved by subsequent generations. Even the apple tree above her grave has been replaced as it grew and decayed. This is as it should be for Ruth is the direct ancestor of most of the well known Marriage families still living in the district.

It must be mentioned that there is another very important grave outside hallowed ground. This is the Saxon burial excavated in 1894 which brought to light one of the most interesting Saxon burials ever found in Britain. The great Saxon chief had been cremated in his coffin and his shield and sword were placed beside his remains, along with all the paraphernalia required for his journey into the next world, including decorative objects in gold and precious stones. It was all found in a gravel pit just behind Clobb's Row where Mr David Christy farmed.

This reminds me of old Charlie Sweeting, an honest Broomfield farm labourer who died in 1913, but whose features are recorded for ever in a wonderful photograph which is itself seventy years old and preserved by lucky chance in the library. He worked for Mr James Christy at The Warren and later for his son at Priors. In his last days just before the First World War he lived in one of the village almshouses and finally died at his great-niece's house in Patching Hall Lane. The photograph shows him under a hedge at Daffy Wood, just about to eat his "beever" of bread and cheese—beever is an old Essex word for elevenses. But Charlie Sweeting, bless him, worked from dawn to dusk and he was having his beever when most people were thinking about breakfast.

There are other Broomfield people living in the older cottages with their tiny windows and their big, black ranges who remember the village much as it was in Charlie's day. One lady in School Lane remembered the hot, dry summer when all the wells dried up and only the pond near the school held water. Then the school kids took their buckets to school and brought home the water at lunchtime and in the evening. Funny to think that fifty years ago a piped water supply was more of a luxury than colour television is today!

30

Charlie Sweeting enjoying his "beever" or "elevenses" in 1900.

In the Museum there is a valuable Sunderland lustre-ware jug which has inscribed on it, "Charles Parsons, Broomfield, Essex, September 27th 1835". It is a souvenir of a visit to Sunderland where the iron bridge over the river was the local landmark and it is also shown on the jug. I looked into this inscription and found that Charles was the son of the local baker and the family bakery was kept by Parsons from at least 1820 right down to recent times when a later Charlie pushed his handcart round the lanes with the bread he had just baked that day.

I hope these bits and pieces about Broomfield will serve to make my point—that history is the doings of people—and that people are lovable and interesting for themselves. Broomfield owes its history to the lively villagers of the twentieth century as much as to the dead Saxons of the ninth.

31

CHAPTER FOUR

On Through the District of Braintree

FROM Chelmsford to Boreham, which is not far along the track of the old Roman road, one passes, on the left, the restored gatehouses marking the drive to New Hall. It is not open to public view, being now a convent and private girls' school and, large though the present building is, it is but a small part of the splendid mansion built for Henry VIII about 1520 and called Beaulieu.

The county historian D. W. Coller claims "New Hall, Boreham, however, was the most remarkable residence of Henry VIII in Essex, both from its own splendour and the historical connection it has with the brilliant life and bloody death of the fair Anne Boleyn, who, from the possessions of her family, and her own abode at Rochford Hall and elsewhere, may be considered a daughter of this county."

New Hall, in fact, belonged originally to her father, Sir Thomas Boleyn. Though it passed out of royal ownership in 1573 its continuing importance can be judged from its sale to George Villiers, Duke of Buckingham, for £30,000 in 1620. Yet some thirty years later it was sold for but five shillings. This was because the Villiers estates were confiscated when the family supported the King in the Civil War, and in 1651 New Hall was bought by Cromwell for that nominal sum. However, Oliver preferred Hampton Court and so exchanged the one for the other. The place came back to the Villiers at the Restoration and was soon bought for General Monck, who rode the storms of the Civil War to be a major architect of the Restoration. His work was rewarded with a peerage and a pension of £7,000 a year. He lived in New Hall on a lavish scale and Charles II was a frequent visitor. His son Christopher entertained James II there in 1686.

The old house survived intact until the middle of the eighteenth century when about nine-tenths of the ageing fabric was demolished by the then owner John Olmius, " . . . yet reserving sufficient of it to make a noble and commodius county seat for himself, to which he added several new offices."

The story of its life from 1798 is bound up in the saga of the struggles of a small religious foundation, the Canonesses of the order of the Holy Sepulchre at Liege, to find a home where they would be free to practice their beliefs. They came here, and stayed in peace. The convent school they established has a wide reputation. Any girl who attends it should be good at English history for many of the kings and queens of this country have trodden where she studies.

The Boreham airfield once heard the throb of American bombers, but now it echoes to the sound of motor engines as the Ford Motor Company carries out hush-hush trials on this converted proving ground. When the airfield was being levelled it was said that a bulldozer broke open the grave of a witch, marked by an old stone, and the local papers record a series of agricultural setbacks at that time, which were attributed to the witch's vengeful curses. There was a witch who was hanged and buried at Boreham. The entry in the church register can be seen today, "1593. July 29. Mother Haven suffered at Boreham for witchcraft." The "H" placed in the margin opposite this entry probably indicates that the corpse was buried outside the churchyard in unconsecrated ground.

Further along the road past New Hall and on the other side, Ford's Mechanised Farming Centre occupies Boreham House. It was built in 1728 with, it is said, material obtained from the great demolition of New Hall. It was then the home of the Tyrell family and continued so until the last male representative of that ancient line died at the House in 1877. The saloon and entrance hall reflect that original splendour and the external view is just as impressive with its long drives either side of an ornamental lake.

Boreham's true centre was not even on the old main road, now shouldered aside by the three-lane highway. Old inns like the *Cock* were there to catch the travelling trade, but the church of St Andrew and the village school are down the turning by the *Red Lion*, where they are kept company by a group of lovingly restored sixteenth century houses. The Vicar here had the painful task of identifying and reburying several human skulls and other bones found in a recent building operation. It would seem that even before written record the churchyard was extended beyond its present limits. But one tomb that cannot be missed stands in the church, a grand three-figured monument to successive Earls of Sussex who inhabited New Hall from Elizabethan times. Round the bend Old Hall still stands while Boreham Hall, as it is known today, is tucked away in the fields on the right.

Next, northeast, lies Hatfield Peverel where a priory was established by William Peverel in the twelfth century. William's mother was Ingelrica, the daughter of a noble Saxon whose beauty brought her to the eye of William the Conqueror and she became his mistress. Later she married one of his knights, Ralph Peverel, and regretting, in her old age, her past behaviour she founded a college for secular canons and entered its rule herself, finally to be buried in its chapel. Her son William converted the college to a Benedictine priory and endowed it further with much property but its glory was eclipsed at the Dissolution. The whole of the present parish church is but the nave of the priory church, with two aisles added later. That is why today's church seems strangely off the village centre.

Hatfield Peverel has a place in English history as the home of several witches. Upon their examination at the Assize in Chelmsford in 1566, Elizabeth Francis, Mother Agnes Waterhouse and her daughter Joan were subjected to questioning by lawyers and judges who believed absolutely that these poverty-stricken, uneducated countrywomen could have power vested in them by the devil. Mother Waterhouse was hanged.

At the beginning of the nineteenth century the villagers founded the Friendly Society at the *Crown Inn*. This early sickness benefit society carried on right down to the eighteen-fifties when it was absorbed into the Witham Permanent Building Society.

Miller Christy's book on Essex trade signs states: "The sign of the Crown is very common in Essex, occurring twenty-eight times altogether . . . We read of it as early as 1467, when a certain Walter Walters, who kept the Crown in Cheapside, made an innocent Cockney pun, saying that he would make his son heir to the Crown, which so displeased his gracious Majesty, King Edward IV, that he ordered the man to be put to death for high treason." That was interesting but what about this particular crown?

I discovered the ownership of a pair of cottages in 1607 which by 1641 were the subject of a court action because of the "enlarging of rooms . . . and receiving of inmates". The inn had begun, and was known as "the Drume" though it changed its name to the *Crown* by 1688 and its latest restoration and refurnishing was in 1973.

The Hatfield Peverel Cavalry, according to the local paper for 1803, were reviewed, with other Essex troops, by the Duke of York on Galleywood Common. Hatfield Peverel also had its own ghost—Shaen's Shaggy Dog. This beast haunted the grounds of Crix, the big house owned by the Shaens in the last two centuries. It is said to have been inoffensive unless attacked, when its fury knew no bounds. The driver of a two-horse wagon went for the dog one night with his whip; and driver, horses, cart and all were reduced to a heap of smoking ashes.

The River Ter which flows through this place gives its name to the neighbouring village of Terling which I was told to pronounce like "darling". It is like a dream to slide away down the side road that leads on through the rich farmland where hedges, fields and trees in any season of the year give solid proof that Essex is a fertile and well-cared for county. In the valley the Ter runs into a wide pool where graceful trees are reflected in the mirror surface. Up the hill there comes into view one of the finest approaches to a village in the whole county. The cottages on the left, and the old Manor House, keep their condition through the loving attention of the proud owners. Standing amongst oak and elm is the church whose tower of warm, red brick has been a landmark for well over two hundred years.

Sundial on the tower of All Saints, Terling.

"The delightful pink and white washed houses". ▶

Behind the church is Terling Place, home of the Strutt family, presently the Lords Rayleigh who have been famous in literature, science and agriculture. They were people of importance in Terling from about 1720, building their present home from 1765 and adding the wings in 1820. The peerage was granted for the squire's services to the Essex militia in the opening years of the nineteenth century. He was such a humble man that he declined the honour, but his wife accepted it in her name that it might be passed on to their son. She took Rayleigh for the title because the family owned property there.

John William Strutt, third Baron Rayleigh (1842-1919), was a renowned mathematician and physicist who won the Nobel Prize for physics in 1904. He gave that prize, worth £8,000, towards an extension of the famous Cavendish Laboratory at Cambridge. Sir William Addison in his "Essex Worthies" says of him, " . . . Apart from his skill in research, Lord Rayleigh had a remarkable gift for organising existing knowledge, and it was this gift that led to another enterprise, not normally associated with science—the Lord Rayleigh's Dairies. This was based on his calculations of the milk needed for its scientific supply to the rapidly expanding population of London. Under the management of his brother, the Hon. E. G. Strutt, he built up a fine herd of between 1,400 and 1,500 cattle at the farm at Terling and opened eight dairy shops in London."

It is said that the fourth Baron Rayleigh fell into an argument with Sir Oliver Lodge, the pioneer in psychic research, over the possibility of communicating with the dead. Sir Oliver called for a gas jar from the laboratory at Terling Place, and sealed within it a blank piece of paper and a pencil. He declared that when he died he would prove the existence of an after life by causing the pencil to write a message on the paper. He died in 1940, but the paper remains unmarked in the gas jar on the shelf in the laboratory to this day. As the fourth Baron died in 1947 it may be that the argument has been settled amicably elsewhere!

The village has delightful pink and white washed houses, one of the longest fords in Essex and what was, I remember, a black rotting old windmill. Now that windmill is a brilliant white and has been transformed into a home as modern as it is unusual.

Witham is a very pleasant place to park the car and shop at leisure. At Newlands, for instance, there is a new, small shopping arcade adjacent to an extensive car park with a children's playground immediately to hand.

Today the bypass takes the ever increasing load of through traffic out of sight and hearing making it possible to pause in Newland Street and appreciate that above the flashy modern facades of the shops are the clues to the true age of these old buildings. Dorothy L. Sayers, the great detective story writer, lived in one of the Georgian fronted cottages. One of the more modern roads is called Dorothy Sayers Drive and recent projects like Wimsey Court and Vane Court bear the names of characters in her famous books. Sadly a lot of the old buildings are coming down to make room for these later developments, and evidence of Witham's history is rapidly disappearing.

All those Georgian-looking houses in Newland Street are not just piecemeal development. Behind these frontages many a house or cottage dates back much further in the details of its construction, but in the eighteenth century a chalybeate spring, one of those mineral-bearing fountains which made Bath famous, was discovered in Witham, and plans were set in hand to turn the place into a grand spa. Sadly, though the spring was there to fill a thousand cups, the carriages of the better classes just never arrived, and Witham stayed a market town where farmers gathered to sell their produce to the London markets.

The settlers of the iron age left their mark in the form of tin coins which circulated amongst the ancient Britons of Witham, and in the slight remains of their circular huts which were first put up more than two thousand years ago.

The Romans have left, in plenty, more sophisticated and significant evidence of their occupation of this place.

When it comes to the Saxons we get the first written record of the town still existing. It is a passage in the *Anglo-Saxon Chronicle* written in 913 A.D: "Between Rogation day and Midsummer King Edward went with part of his forces to Maldon in Essex, and encamped there whilst the earthwork at Witham was being built and stockaded . . ." The Saxons had found their way to Witham across the sea and up the Blackwater to its junction with the river Brain, known to folk of an earlier generation as the Guith, from which Guithavon Street took its name, or the Podsbrook. Early and continuous settlement had forced the forest back and Saxon immigrants could see the value of this gentle hill in the bend of the river, which looked as easily defended a place as you could find, so boats were drawn up, and all hands were set to pushing out the Romano-British settlers and bringing to Witham the Saxon way of life. Swords into ploughshares made sense in this fertile river valley and down to our days Witham fields have become famous for specialised seed production.

About a hundred and fifty years after that entry in the *Anglo-Saxon Chronicle* the Saxons in their turn were being dispossessed by the Normans, who were authors of the next written record to mention Witham by name, the Domesday Book of 1086.

The place had been divided by Saxon lords into the "manors" of Bennington Hall, Blunts Hall, Howbridge Hall, Powers Hall and Witham itself. It says much for our stable British way of life that the sites of two of those old manors still have houses on them, carrying the same names through a thousand years.

The Spread Eagle, Witham.   *Owen Keen*

From that time on we shall find reflections of passing time in the parish church of St Nicholas which stands on Chipping Hill in the oldest part of the town, near those ancient earthworks through which the railway now runs. Chipping is a development of "cheaping", the old English word for a market. The right to hold a market on this spot was granted to the Knights Templars who came into possession of the manor some time after the Conquest. In the church the south doorway harks back to the twelfth century, the fine tower was probably begun in the thirteenth century and the four-arch arcades between nave and aisles are relics of the fourteenth century. No doubt the continuing maintenance and adornment of the church was the result of increasing prosperity in Witham as it became a centre for the sale of wool from the large flocks of sheep then being herded in Essex, and from the number of weavers who set up in the town at this time, producing cloth which went all over Europe. This may have been the reason for the erection of the wonderfully carved rood screen separating the choir from the congregation, in the fifteenth century. That screen had already been up a hundred years when a grand gathering of gentry and nobility came to the funeral of John Southcote, a justice of the Queen's Bench who died in 1585. His tomb, with his wife laid beside him, is marked by their effigies on the tomb chest, interesting to modern visitors for its faithful reproduction of the costume of the time.

The memory of the cloth trade and the market is preserved in the sight of the old guildhall nearby, and the inn next to the churchyard, the *Woolpack*. It is a long time since I called on the widowed landlady who proved such a mine of information on things Essex. She showed me how the inn had so outgrown itself in extensions down the years that an outside Tudor window is now an interior feature of one of the bedrooms. Round about there are several old timber-framed and plastered houses to delight the eye. One opposite the church has so curious a finial to the great chimney stack, only revealed upon recent restoration, that it was at first thought to be a wayside shrine!

From this essentially medieval atmosphere it is but a step back to the Georgian facades of Newland Street where shops and offices are incorporated in old buildings too numerous for me to give separate attention, though the inns, the *Spread Eagle* and the *White Hart* must be mentioned, for they are both excellent places at which to find refreshment, especially for an evening out.

There is a side road to Braintree which follows the west bank of the River Brain, and leads through to Faulkbourne where you will see a pond which is a very important part of that village. It is a wishing well developed from the old holy well. Water was as essential to early man as fire and he founded his religion on such essential gifts of nature. The god of the spring had to be placated if he was to supply a never-failing fountain of life-supporting water. And if the water did fail then ancient man was sure it was the god's anger, rather than a natural cause which he could not comprehend. In the Middle Ages, this well, dedicated, like the church, to the missionary Bishop, St German, became quite famous for its curative powers—or as a "wishing well" for pilgrims between Bury St Edmunds and Canterbury who went out of their way specially to visit it.

The church of St German was built by the Normans to serve the settlement of Falcheburna, as they called it in the Domesday Book, or Folk's Stream as some scholars have interpreted it today. That is, the stream of life which, through common need was common property even in the dawn of history. So hallowed was the spot that Christian missionaries realised it was the best place in which to build their own church to ensure its due reverence from pagan half-believers. Today you can walk through the churchyard under the graceful wrought iron arch that supports a lantern and up to the little church porch, in red brick, added long after pilgrims ceased to pass this way, but so mellowed by time that it harmonises perfectly with the grey rubble walls that the Normans first erected. The sombre green of a yew or two is a foil to the grey of the church with its weathered tiles and its grey, shingled spire rising above the small belfry. Inside, there are some very old benches, some unusual architecture and the view of an ancient "helm," part of a coat of armour, on the chancel wall. In a village church like this you find a very real feeling with people of the past as you look around at the evidence all about of folk coming here to worship in peace and friendliness together for a thousand years or more.

From the churchyard there is a lovely view across acres of parkland dotted with clumps of tall trees to the red walls of Faulkbourne Hall. I saw it all in a tremulous haze of a hot summer's day, when the cattle had drawn in groups to the trees' shade and the walls of the Hall shimmered like a mirage. I was quite alone in the churchyard and there was not one person to be seen in the whole, wide-ranging, glorious view. That was an experience from which in retrospect I still draw great pleasure.

I found a path that led to the drive which ran on into the distance up to the Hall, a long drive which meant that the Hall must remain, as far as this ordinary member of the public was concerned, but a mansion in a mirage. The sight of a lodge house nearby, all alone in a green wilderness, was in itself, evidence of greater glory down the drive—for so it is. Faulkbourne has been described as "the most impressive fifteenth century brick mansion in the county."

This lovely, rambling mansion began as an earlier timber-framed house in true Essex tradition, of which there are remnants to be seen in the structure today. When the place came to Sir John Montgomery he obtained a "licence to crenellate" around 1439; that is, permission from the King to fortify his house with towers and battlements. So the house as we see it today was begun, and the building proceeded as the family became wealthier and more notable in our county's story. During the lifetime of Sir Thomas Montgomery, who died in 1494, the area covered by the Hall was virtually doubled with all the new building. The Fortescues followed him at the Hall, to be succeeded in turn by the Bullocks, from 1637. This family continued at the Hall for hundreds of years, and their family memorials are some of the most splendid ornaments in the church. The Hall did not change much—it took families in and sheltered them, and watched their generations rise to fame and sink to obscurity as the line ran out, only to see the cycle begin again. The Fortescues changed the place very little, but the wealthy Bullocks made a number of alterations and additions to give the Hall its rambling magnificence of today, and all, surprisingly in good red brick. In 1897 the Bullocks sold up and the house was eventually purchased by the Parkers whose progeny still live there.

In the meadows behind the hall the River Brain meanders, and the lane reflects those twists and turns, a track hammered out by travellers in far-off days when the river was a real barrier and its threatening floods in winter set the pathway at a safe distance from its banks. Past the church where the road bends you will come across the little collection of houses, old and new, which make up the village.

The old house on the right with a window quite low on the side was once Faulkbourne post office. Although the house has been restored extensively there is one feature which has been retained. By the bedroom window there is a hatch or shutter because when the stage came clattering through in the dead of a winter's night, the village postmaster had to get up, go downstairs, unbolt all the doors and stand in his nightgown in the chilling wind while the coachman handed down the post for the village. Therefore, the Faulkbourne post master had this little door built right beside his bed which was below the window. Stage coaches were tall old things and when the coach came by the coachman simply had to bang on the hatch and the postmaster would slide it open to receive the midnight mail. I am grateful to my friend, Maurice Smith, of Witham for this interesting detail of Essex history.

The Notley villages, Black and White, offer pleasant enough countryside and, in their churches, unusual features on which to ponder. Black Notley, well-known to many people for its large hospital, is also known around the world because of John Ray who was born here in 1627 to the wife of the village blacksmith.

He obtained a rudimentary education at Braintree Grammar School, then but a converted chapel in the parish church. This enabled him to go on to Trinity College, Cambridge. His cleverness was already evident. He was eventually elected a Fellow and continued at the College for eighteen years. The subject which occupied his intellect and his life was natural history. Today there are books enough to identify every animal and plant, setting each in a classification which makes its origin and relationship clear. In the seventeenth century the knowledge of natural history was scanty, fact and fiction were hopelessly mixed together. John Ray set himself to put order in man's recording of his natural surroundings, particularly in the field of botany. His enthusiasm is shown in his first book, the *Catalogus Cantabrigiam* of 1660. It is a list of plants he had found in his walks about the College and can be claimed to be our first local "flora". At the same time he continued to study languages to the point where he was able not only to write his books and letters in the customary Latin, but also to communicate with correspondents in their own language.

It was the religious intolerance of the time which brought his happy college life to an end and caused him to return to his native village, from whence he set out on his botanical tours with a wealthy friend and former pupil, Francis Willoughby. They planned to compile together a classification of plant and animal life, Ray describing and ordering plant life. They were indefatigable in an age of primitive means of travel in penetrating the length and breadth of our country. Ray's notes are not dry as dust but show what a warm-hearted witty man he was, able to get on with all kinds of people and find profit in their conversation. With the nationalist spirit much in evidence today it is apt that Ray should have reported three hundred years ago that the Scots "cannot endure to hear their country or countrymen spoken against."

Though Ray had little money at this time good friends helped him to tour Europe in further study of its flora. He married in 1671 and was saddened a year later by the death of his friend and collaborator Willoughby, whose work he patiently finished and edited. From his small home at Black Notley with his wife and four daughters, where he could not visit he could write, and he did. Scholars all over the world sent not only letters for his opinion and advice, but also parcels of specimens. All the time John Ray was working on his great book, the *History of Plants* which was published in three volumes in 1686, 1688 and 1704. From all his travels and correspondence he was able to classify and describe more than eleven thousand species. His system of classification was so useful that his book continued as the standard book of reference for over two centuries. His profit on this amazing work was just £5! He died in 1705, in his seventy-eighth year. It has been said of him, "he found Nature a trackless wilderness, but his genius and perseverance reduced her beauties to a methodical plan."

Though his work did not profit him greatly, it was recognized in his time and is acknowledged in the lavish Latin inscription on his tomb in the churchyard at Black Notley, which was erected at the sole cost of the Bishop of London. An English translation of a small part of that inscription runs:

"Hid in this narrow tomb, this marble span,
Lies all that death could snatch from this great man;
His body moulders in its native clay,

While o'er wide worlds his works their beams display,
As bright and everlasting as the day.
To those just fame ascribes immortal breath,
And in his writings he outlives his death."

From Witham it is but a few miles up the road to Kelvedon, the next settlement. The main A12 must be used, with a weather eye kept for the slip road. On the way one passes through Rivenhall End, the extension of the little village of Rivenhall which lies up a lane to the northwest. It is the site of a Roman occupation which has never been fully investigated but which was further indicated by an excavation under the very walls of the church when it was being restored recently. Evidence was produced of worship on that site through Saxon and Norman times, but the great glory of the church of St Mary and All Saints today is the rare, thirteenth century stained glass rescued in recent times from a decaying French church and reset here by a former incumbent.

Rivenhall Place, much further up the lane, has grounds planned by Humphry Repton, the great landscape gardener. Hogarth is said to have stayed here frequently when commissioned to paint the portraits of the Western family, of whom more later. Just a little distance on is the village within a village called Silver End. It was created by Francis Henry Crittall who developed his father's ironmongery business into the great Crittall Manufacturing Company of 1889 which made metal window frames. He was anxious that his workers should be decently housed in pleasant surroundings and had his chance in 1926, when the firm also introduced a factory to be run by disabled men. Modern times have seen a change in working conditions, travel has become so much easier and many people own their own homes, so the estate was less and less needed and has been sold. Francis Crittall takes his place in industrial history as the first employer to introduce the five day working week.

Perhaps the greatest claim to fame that Rivenhall may be allowed is that it was the place of birth of Thomas Tusser in 1523. He could be called the Farmer's Poet. In various moves about the country he tried the farming life and distilled his experiences into a very long poem entitled "The Hundreth Good Pointes of Husbandrie" which came out in 1557. In 1573 it was expanded to five hundred "good pointes". In it he introduces himself:

"It came to pass that born I was
Of lineage good, of gentle blood,
In Essex layer, in village fair,
That Rivenhall hight:
Which village lied by Banktree side;
There spend did I my infancy,
There then my name, in honest fame
Remained in sight."

Then he goes on to give sound advice to farmers and housekeepers through each season of the year.

"Green rye in September when timely thou hast
October for weat sowing calleth as fast.

If weather will suffer, this council I geve,
Leave sowing of wheat before Hallowmas eve."

Poor man, he died in a debtors' prison in 1580. Fuller, in his *Worthies of England* sums up Tusser's life rather sadly: " . . . he spread his bread with all sorts of butter, yet none would stick thereon."

The architecture of Kelvedon village street is fascinating in its variety. There are still so many points of similarity with the photographs taken before 1870 by Lord Western's bailiff with what is reputed to have been the first camera used in Essex.

Kelvedon High Street in 1870.

The Western family contribute a large part to the story of this locality. The Essex connection began in 1692 when the London merchant Thomas Western bought Rivenhall Place from the Wisemans. It faltered for a while when one after another of the heirs died in quick succession, five of them in fact in the twenty-five years up to 1733. One of the family, Shirley Western, was Rector of Rivenhall from 1772 to 1824. The heir who recovered the family fortunes was Charles Callis, Baron Western, 1767-1844, who came into his inheritance when he was just four years old. He was an avid collector, traveller and antiquarian, but his main interest was in the improvement of farming methods. He it was who added Felix Hall to the family estate and thus forged the Kelvedon connection. Here, again the family failed in the immediate line. So it was that Thomas Burch Western of Tattingstone, Suffolk inherited the Essex estate, and armed his bailiff with a camera for our subsequent delight. His grandson Charles Callis Western, third baronet, died in 1917 without issue, and the Essex Western story ended.

A native of the village who became known throughout the world was Charles Haddon Spurgeon, a great man of the Victorian age. He was a chapel preacher, son and grandson of men of the same bent. His power as a preacher in London in 1854 is demonstrated by the fact that within a year the chapel had to be enlarged to contain the congregation drawn by his words. Before it was complete it could be seen that it would not suffice for the evergrowing audience. So it was that the Metropolitan Tabernacle on Newington Causeway was built in 1861, to seat six thousand eager chapelgoers. It is said that from then until he died in 1892 the chapel was filled to overflowing every time he preached. An estimated fifty million copies of his sermons were printed for circulation all over the world. On the west side of the High Street a small house bears a plaque which simply states that Charles Haddon Spurgeon was born there on 19th June, 1834.

Coggeshall is the modern rendering of the Old English for "Cocc's nook". It is a charming "nook" today, with the A120 diverted on a new by-pass. The village street is beautiful in the variety of its architecture and the pastel shades of its painted houses. Antique shops and art studios have gathered here in the aesthetic atmosphere. As late as 1755 a woman was buried here as "a reputed witch". The church has survived as a fifteenth century church built as, and remaining, a complete entity. The nave and tower were almost entirely destroyed by a bomb in the Second World War, but were rebuilt in 1956 as a faithful copy of that impressive original and the difference cannot now be detected.

The other notable building on the main street going west is Paycocke's House, now in the care of the National Trust. Thomas Paycocke was son of John who died in 1505 leaving him, "my house lying . . . in the West Street of Coggeshall afore the Vicarage . . ." That house is a fine example of Tudor domestic architecture. The expert, Pevsner, rates it as "one of the most attractive half-timbered houses of England, regardless of the fact that much in its facade is restored." The family's merchant mark is evident in the rich carving. It is an ermine's tail, which must have been repeated thousands of times on the bales of cloth which made Thomas Paycocke so wealthy. The particular cloth called "Coxhall whites" made the whole village a prosperous centre of the great East Anglian cloth trade.

Coggeshall has also gathered to itself down the years a legendary reputation for odd happenings, called "Coggeshall jobs". It is said, for example, that when the church clock struck only eleven times at midday, and the villagers heard that at nearby Lexden the clock struck two at one o'clock, one of their number was despatched to Lexden with a pony and trap to bring back the missing stroke. In the eighteenth century, when so many men answered the call to arms against Napoleon, the Coggeshall lads were not to be outdone. They formed their own band of Volunteers. There was but one snag, nobody wanted to be a common soldier, so everybody in the Coggeshall Volunteers was an officer! Going west along the A120 we arrive at Braintree and Bocking.

The Braintree drinking fountain, erected in 1882 by George Courtauld.

The name Courtauld is almost synonymous with this place and it all began with a Huguenot refugee bringing his son Augustine to England in the seventeenth century. Essex connections date from his great-grandson George, born in 1761. He ventured into silk-throwing, setting up his first mill at Pebmarsh in 1798, later moving to a larger mill at Bocking. His son Samuel, born in 1793, stayed in Essex when the family emigrated to Ohio in America. Up to his death in 1881 his was the energy and inspiration which developed the company out of all recognition. By 1846 he was entertaining 1600 employees to a special dinner and by 1861 nearly double that number were employed. Sir Samuel Courtauld was the man who founded the Courtauld Institute of Art in 1931. His only daughter was the first wife of Lord Butler of Saffron Walden. She died in 1954.

It was not until 1934 that the two parishes of Braintree and Bocking were amalgamated into one urban district. Braintree was occupied from prehistoric times, as proved by finds of flint tools and bronze weapons in the silt which dammed the Brain at Skitts Hill to form a lake over which a community lived in timber huts erected on stilts. A Roman hoard of three thousand coins found in the town, together with burial urns, continues evidence of occupation.

The old roads tramped by Roman feet came into their own again a thousand years later when Essex folk in Christian piety began making pilgrimages to holy places. Many a band of pilgrims made its way from London through Essex to Suffolk, where the royal and saintly shrine at Bury St Edmunds brought an endless throng of visitors, and to Norfolk, where the shrine of Our Lady of Walsingham was the goal. Braintree stood in the right spot to receive these pilgrims, to put them up for the night, to provide food and drink and replacement of shoes and dress. Braintree's inns, and its shops, have an ancient and honourable place in the town's history.

It was as early as 1199 that the Bishop of London, as Lord of the Manor, obtained a charter from King John to establish a weekly market and a fair. In Tudor times when religious belief was oppressive a wave of immigrants from the low countries brought to Braintree their weaving skill, supplementing the industry known to have existed here from early times.

In the Essex Record Office can be seen the documents which take up the later story, from the "Parish Book" starting in 1581 to the "Minutes of the Four and Twenty", an early kind of town council which endlessly elected itself without reference to the townspeople, so that from 1619 to 1712 the town was run by a group of dictators whose activity was only ended by a direct order from Quarter Sessions.

Courtauld benefactions which, by their very architecture, have changed the face, and the life, of the town, include the town hall built and furnished by Sir William in 1938, and the clock in its central tower with five bells. The hospital too was presented to the town in 1921. The splendid fountain with the bronze figure of a boy holding a fish, placed in the foreground to the old church is another bequest. The church of St Michael's is an island of fifteenth century peace in a river of twentieth century traffic. Roman brick in the older parts, like the thirteenth century tower, indicates the early foundation of St Michael's at the very heart of the little settlement. Yet even in this ancient pile the Courtaulds have made their contribution in the form of the electric clock in the tower. The south chapel offers visitors a rich reward in the carving of its roof timbers, and other points of interest range in age through a thousand years. Famous men have walked about here, like Nicholas Udall, born 1506, who was the author of the first regular English comedy, called *Ralph Roister Doister*. He was vicar here from 1537 to 1544.

The town centre was described in 1831 as follows: "What remains of the old town of Braintree, which forms the central part, consists of several streets irregularly formed and inconveniently narrow; many of the houses are ancient, and some of them built of wood; but in the great thoroughfare street, and other parts of these combined towns, there are many capital houses belonging to opulent tradespeople . . . " Things have not changed all that much in a hundred years. The recently introduced one-way system has made it a little easier for the motorist to thread his way through the town centre, where those old houses can still be seen, including several of the inns which filled the town's ancient role as a traveller's rest.

Old print of Braintree market, 1826.

Where Braintree merges imperceptibly into Bocking at Bradford Street one can sense the atmosphere of an old print. It is unfortunate that some of the old buildings are deteriorating, in one case at least so that its site may be commercially exploited. But there is a commercial building of earlier days which has become an object of beauty and interest in Bocking. It is the old post mill in Church Street which has been carefully restored and is open on certain days to the public. An intriguing collection of old farm implements is being gathered there. The church of St Mary, founded in 995, has a nave and a splendid east window dating from the thirteenth century; and further embellishments presented by the Courtaulds.

Rayne achieved national headlines as the scene of the gruesome Barn murder case. The Barn restaurant lies between Braintree, which used to be called Great Rayne, and Little Rayne itself, on the A120. The severity of the plague in 1666 brought death and suffering to many families. I like the paragraph in the church guide which runs: "Except for the Rector, the Rev. Richard Kidder, there were no famous inhabitants. He regarded his stay at Rayne as 'the lost part' of his life and he described the local people as being 'factious to the last degree.' But even if he was not on good terms with his parishioners, at least he had the leisure to write some of the many books and sermons that made his name well known." He went on to become Bishop of Bath and Wells.

There is a charming legend which, in early days, made All Saints the object of pilgrimage. A local lady of high standing, Margaret de Naylinghurst, was having a difficult time in labour. Her servants were sent to pray to our Lady of Mercy in the church for a safe delivery. They swore they saw the lips of the statue move in seraphic smile and on their return they found that the baby had been born and mother and

46

child were well. So expectant mothers, and barren wives, came here to pray and newly weds were told the old Essex saying that they would "go ere long and say your prayers at Rayne." The church survived in its Norman building of 1199, with a tower of red brick added by the Capell family in 1510, until 1840, when the body of the building was in such a bad way that it was entirely rebuilt. The tower remained, however, and its one-handed clock is an interesting feature.

In a glass case under the tower is preserved a knight's helm. It is only a copy, but it tells of an interesting story. Sir Giles Capell, Lord of the Manor, was one of the Knights who, led by Henry VIII, challenged all comers from the continent for thirty days at the Field of the Cloth of Gold in 1520. In his will he wrote: "I will that my beste helmett and my armyng Sworde be sett over my funeralls according to the devise of the harrauld." They remained in position over his tomb in the church until the 1840 restoration, when the Capell tombs were unaccountably destroyed and the armour was removed by the builder. The helm was sold to Miss Courtauld for ten shillings and she gave it to a friend who sold it for a great sum to an American. It is now one of the prized exhibits of the Metropolitan Museum of Art in New York.

Having mentioned the pilgrim traffic which helped found townships like Braintree, let me draw your attention to Great Leighs, and its inn, *St Anne's Castle,* which is said to be the oldest licensed public house in England. In medieval times it is thought to have been a hermitage. It was the resting of those pilgrims and their refreshment on their way to Canterbury which brought the business which continues today. While in this place we can connect again with history and people through the person of Arthur Wilson, who lived at Pond Park, Little Leighs, and died in 1652. His contemporary account of the trial of witches brings the horror story to modern eyes, and his *History of Great Britain, Being the Life and Reign of King James the First* was published just after his death. As gentleman-in-waiting to the third Earl of Essex he was much concerned with current affairs in our county and this is reflected in his writings.

It should not be forgotten that Leez Priory, Little Leighs, was built as a home for the famous Lord Rich, on the site of the priory dissolved and demolished around 1537. It was in its turn largely knocked down, but the impressive gatehouse and parts of the outer quadrangle remain.

CHAPTER FIVE

Colchester and the Constable Country

COLCHESTER has been the subject of several books in itself and there is a mine of fascinating information in the local collection in the district library.

To appreciate the town one must walk and the best place to start a circumnabulation is at the top of the High Street. Here the disused water tower looms on its four tall brick legs and is called "Jumbo" by the locals, from the name of a famous elephant in the eighteen-nineties when it was built. For sheer bulk it cannot come up to that of the Balkerne Gate ruins. The public house, formerly and most aptly called the *Hole in the Wall*, is built into it and so obscures the Roman plan by occupying one of the original thoroughfares. A true picture of this fortified Roman gate can be seen in the excellent model in the Colchester and Essex Museum housed in the castle at the bottom of the hill. In this well run museum the wonderful story of this the oldest town in Britain can clearly be traced.

The Hole in the Wall, before road alterations.

Colchester's name could derive from the Saxon for a fortress on the river Colne, or from the "Colonia fortress", the far more ancient settlement of veteran Roman soldiers in the first Roman colony in this country, founded around 50 A.D. But Colchester was famous long before the Romans came marching through the Essex forests. It was then the great capital of the kingdoms of south east Britain and was named after the Celtic war god Camulos, which the Romans translated to Camulodunum. Cunobelin, better known, through Shakespeare, as Cymbeline, was ruling when the Romans arrived. Some people think it was his great burial mound in Lexden Park which produced the rich evidence of that age now to be seen in the museum.

It is in the museum that the life and times of that later Roman Colchester can best be imagined. The castle is built on the remains of a Roman temple raised to celebrate the victories of the emperor-invader Claudius. The Norman keep is bigger than that in the Tower of London. It was put out of action by Cromwell's men and later sold to a scrap merchant who started to demolish it to sell the stone; but the very bulk and strength of the building was too much for him and he had to give up. There is a bookstall in the Museum where a guide to the architecture and contents of the place is available as well as much other interesting local material.

The constant increase in traffic even before the internal combustion engine caused the demolition of all the Roman gates except the Balkerne. That name implies "blocking-up". It seems the Saxons completely blocked off this gateway in their efforts to protect the town from Danish raiders. The perpetual closing of that highway saved the gate and so we can still admire it today. The ramparts of the ancient British settlement are still evident in Castle Park where an obelisk marks the spot where the Royalist leaders of the troops besieged by Cromwell's forces were taken out and summarily shot.

There are so many other places of interest to the visitor. Holly Trees, a beautiful Georgian house close to the castle, is now a museum housing a really interesting collection of later antiquities. Across the road the natural history museum is contained in the former, ancient parish church of All Saints. Round the corner, down East Hill and over the river stands the Siege House, a late fifteenth century house, much restored. It however still bears the bullet marks of that ghastly siege whilst Parliamentary troops were winning Colchester from the Royalists during the Civil War. On the way the visitor passes the Minories, a late Georgian house with a wing two hundred years older. It was rebuilt in 1776 by Thomas Boggis, a bay (baize) maker who was mayor of the town in that year. Colchester bays and says were types of cloth woven locally which brought prosperity to the town as its major industry. The house was opened to the public as an art gallery in 1958 as a memorial to Victor Batte-Lay who died in 1935. His collection of Georgian furniture, pictures, china and silver is displayed on the ground floor along with Colchester made clocks from the Bernard Mason collection. The prize exhibits from an Essex point of view are the portraits and drawings by John Constable together with some personal relics of that great artist.

Full justice to this ancient town cannot be done in this book. The flow of history over prehistoric ramparts, Roman walls, Saxon fortifications, Norman castle, Tudor houses, all exposed to Parliamentary artillery and time's indifference, makes a tale of people and their doings which would put to shame most of the novels in the public library.

Boadicea, great warrior queen of the Iceni, had her contribution to the Colchester scene summed up by the historian D. W. Coller of a century ago:

"In time the tyranny of the Romans led to a terrible effort to throw off their yoke, of which Essex was the scene. The King of the Iceni, the people who inhabited Suffolk and Norfolk, and part of Cambridgeshire, appears to have retained his kingdom under the protection of the conquerors; and when he died he left half of his territory and his treasures to the Romans, under the impression that the other half would be secured for his family. The Romans, however, seized the whole. Boadicea, the widow, remonstrated. The extortioners endeavoured to silence her by insult; she was publicly scourged like a common slave, and her daughters were given over to dishonour by the soldiery. This outrage aroused all the spirit of the ancient Briton. The wretched Queen, instead of sinking under her miseries, boldly raised the standard of revolt and vengeance; and fearfully were the Romans made to pay for their breach of faith and want of honesty . . . Tacitus, in his annals, says that the statue of the goddess of Victory at Camulodunum fell down and turned as if yielding to the enemy; howlings were heard in the theatre, and strange noises in the councilhouse; a fearful apparition was seen in the estuary of the Thames towards Mersea Island . . . When, therefore, the Britons, in overwhelming numbers, appeared upon the wooded hills around Colchester, and were joined by the men of Essex, who flocked in thousands to the standard of the Queen, they met with only a feeble resistance. The ninth legion, which had hastened to the rescue, was defeated, and the whole of its infantry slain; and the exasperated Britons swept into the capital of the colony, slaughtering all, even women and children, and mercilessly destroying every object of art and emblem of the Roman sway."

Boadicea's ultimate defeat followed by her self-imposed death is a milestone in British history.

The man who made the most lasting impression on Colchester, even as it stands today, must surely be Eudo Dapifer. As Steward to William the Conqueror until 1087, after his death Eudo brought William Rufus across the Channel to claim the kingdom. For his services he was granted Colchester, in addition to the twenty Essex manors he is shown as owning in the Domesday Book. He set about building a castle with a powerful keep. That keep, known more popularly as the Castle, stands today, shorn of half its bulk but still amazing to the eye. He also had St John's Abbey built in about 1096, and his body was brought back from France to be interred there on his death in 1120.

A great fighter against a later tyranny was John Ball, who came from York to be Rector of St James at Colchester in the fourteenth century. He preached that all men were born equal and his word was like a spark to the tinder of unrest among Essex working men which flamed into the furnace of the Peasants' Revolt of 1381. The awful consequences of that revolt and the fearful retribution exacted by the mighty lords of Essex in the battle at Billericay and the executions at Chelmsford have, thankfully, been forgotten in the long course of English history.

Colchester Castle.

Walter A. Blythin

Later another man questioned the power of the King. Thomas Beche, last Abbot of St John's Abbey, of which only the impressive gateway stands as the entrance to the Garrison Officer's Club, refused to acknowledge the power of Henry VIII above the Pope. The legend has it that the abbot was invited by the King's bailiff to a feast in friendship and on his arrival was served the warrant for his arrest and hurried away to execution at Greenstead.

Holy Trinity church is to be spared the demolition suffered by other redundant churches. This church not only has, in its Roman-brick-sprinkled tower, the only Anglo-Saxon architecture remaining in the town, it also has an interesting monument, which connects with the twentieth century. This memorial survived up to the thorough restoration of the church in 1886 when it was removed from the chancel to the north wall of the north chapel. Its inscription can be translated thus:

51

"Ambrose and William Gilberd erected this monument to William Gilberd, senior, esq., and doctor of physic, in memory of his fraternal affection. He was the eldest son of Jerom Gilberd, Esq., born in the town of Colchester, studied physic at Cambridge, and practised at London more than thirty years, with the greatest applause, and equal success. And being sent for to Court, he was received into the highest favour by Queen Elizabeth, to whom, as also to her successor James, he was principal physician. He wrote a book concerning the magnet, much celebrated by those engaged in nautical affairs. He died in the year of human redemption, 1603, on the last day of November, in the sixty-third year of his age."

This interest in the properties of the magnet was pursued over thirty years before he expressed the results of his research in *De Magnete*. The fundamental contribution made by Gilberd to the modern miracle of electricity has not been fully appreciated in his home town, though a Technical School bears his name. Since the church has now been taken over as an extension of the Museum it is to be hoped that it will be possible to demonstrate Colchester's ancient connection with the electronic age in which we live.

Gilberd was seventeen years old when a Colchester baker named Harsnett was celebrating the birth of a son whom he called Samuel. He was a clever boy who won scholarships to Cambridge colleges and returned to teach at his old Colchester school. In 1597, when thirty-six, he was presented to the living of Chigwell and proceeded from there to the highest ranks in holy orders. He went on to Shenfield and Stisted and was appointed Archdeacon of Essex. He proceeded from bishoprics at Chichester and Norwich to become Archbishop of York in 1629. As a thank offering for this preferment he founded a school at Chigwell, a place which always had a warm place in his heart. He was buried there in 1631 and his grave is marked in the church by a very fine, life-size brass of the Archbishop with cope and mitre. He left his library to Colchester, where it suffered eclipse and despoliation through a hundred years before it was rescued and finally preserved in a special department of Colchester Public Library, where a detailed catalogue is available.

There are so many well-known people connected with Colchester who must be passed over, but in any work touching on the history of the county there is one man who must be mentioned. If you saw the Reverend Philip Morant walking down Colchester High Street today, you would perhaps be startled by his eighteenth century costume, though men's fashions today might render the reverend gentleman's sober garb quite inconspicuous. However, his physical features would set him apart from other men but he is remembered two hundred years after his death for a very good reason.

Philip Morant wrote the first complete history of Essex. Today with the record office and libraries to keep all our county records in good order and easily available it is difficult to imagine the problems that Morant and his less successful predecessors must have had in seeking out the original material.

Morant was born in St Saviour's, Jersey, on 6th October, 1700. His name goes back in Jersey records to 1500. As a boy he spoke the Norman French in which the post-Conquest records of our country were written, and anyone who has attempted to decipher such documents will know that it gave him a headstart. He came to England around 1717 to be educated at Abingdon. He stayed and married, though not until he was thirty-nine, Anne, heiress to Solomon Stebbing of Great Tey. Their union was blessed with but one daughter, who married and had nine children, so that a good number of people today could trace their ancestry back to our eminent historian, one of them being an actor in the well known radio series "The Archers". The young Morant had graduated as a B.A. at Pembroke College, Oxford by 1721 and as an M.A. from Sidney Sussex College, Cambridge in 1729. It was natural in those days that a young man of his standing should think of the church as a career. In 1724 he took up a curacy at Great Waltham, staying for eight years under the Reverend Doctor Nicholas Tindal, who was himself a well known historian.

St Botolph's Priory, Colchester.   *Owen Keen*

He helped Tindal produce for publication a new edition of Rapin's history and wrote some short historical and religious works on his own account. One of these, a riposte to a pamphlet of the day attacking the very fundamentals of the Christian religion, he presented to the Bishop of London. The Bishop, much impressed with the "argumentative power and antiquarian learning" which it displayed, conferred favours on him in the shape of various livings in Essex. So he moved from Shellow Bowells to Broomfield in 1733 then on to Chignall Smealey in 1735, to St Mary-at-the-Walls in Colchester in 1737, to Wickham Bishops in 1742 and finally to Aldham in 1745.

In 1748 the first flowering of his interest in the county was evinced in the publication of the *History and Antiquities of Colchester*. With William Bowyer he risked the printing of just two hundred copies on an advance subscription basis. In this work Morant really showed what a good historian he was, conducting his own research and putting in detail which could hardly be expected.

Twenty years later it was published in a second edition, as the first part of his great work, *The History and Antiquities of the County of Essex* which appeared over the period 1760 to 1768 in the two magnificent volumes which can still be referred to in public libraries all round the county.

There is no doubt that Morant was grateful for the fruits of earlier endeavours in this field. More than a hundred years before him Thomas Jekyll had made certain collections towards such a work. William Holman who died in 1730 used these notes and added his own researches to a manuscript which actually came on his death into the hands of the same Nicholas Tindal under whom Morant served. The manuscript swelled by further contributions passed to Dr Nathaniel Salmon who died in 1742, before he could arrange publication, and so the body of material passed through further hands until it was acquired by Morant himself around 1750. So Philip Morant, by editing this mass of material, adding his own research and rewriting the whole and then seeing it through the press, became the first man to produce a complete county history.

Mr R. Powell, when editor of the massive and definitive but still incomplete *Victoria History of the County of Essex*, which is already in six volumes, addressed a public meeting about the great man and said, with some feeling, "He was a happy man, he finished his job!" That was what previous endeavours had failed to do and we must remember that our historian was nearly sixty when he started. Mr Powell sums up Philip Morant's contribution in this manner: the two-volume history is well-arranged and very easy to use with a good index and with sensible footnotes on the Domesday records quoted. Compared with histories of other counties it comes out very well, and it is still the only large-scale, complete and original history of Essex.

One of the spokes in the wheel of roads which radiate from Colchester is the A137. It runs northeast past Welshwood Park and Fox Street to arrive at Ardleigh. The parish has been changed by the improvement of that important road to Ipswich and the formation of the Ardleigh reservoir, with a big retaining bank 55 feet high, built to hold it off the road and railway north of Moze Hall. The valley from here up to a point just west of the village centre has slowly filled with water from the Salary Brook as it flows from the west and turns south towards the Colne. The Ardleigh Reservoir Order of 1967 set up a scheme which links with the Abberton reservoir in the storage of water from the Great Ouse, transferred and carried along as the augmented flow of the River Stour. It has resulted in a water surface of 150 acres which has made a "V" shape with arms stretching out one and a quarter miles, providing a storage capacity of 482 million gallons by 1971 and allowing a flow into the mains of some 5 million gallons a day in the first stage of development. In 1976 the Essex Water Company announced, "The Ely Ouse Scheme, developed by the Essex River and Great Ouse River Authorities, has reinforced the yield of the Company's other major reservoir at Hanningfield by 56 million gallons per day as well as that of Abberton, and there is potential to increase further the yield by constructing storage for the Ely Ouse water in Suffolk or by utilising the natural underground chalk storage." (Layer-de-la-Haye-Treatment Works. October 1976).

The strange uniqueness of which this place can boast is that the largest Bronze Age cemetery in England has been discovered here by aerial photography and is now being excavated. A Belgic settlement and later, Roman occupation, has been proved by remains of pottery and kilns found a half mile south of the church. In the village, the road by the church of St Mary, the B1029, runs on to Dedham and to Constable country.

The only way to deal with Dedham is to appreciate the artist first, and then its lesser known attractions. John Constable was born in 1776 at East Bergholt on the Suffolk side of the river Stour, but he had to cross the bridge beside the lock to come to school in Dedham, and those journeyings through Essex scenery provided him with inspiration years later as he worked in his London studio. His father, Golding Constable, inherited property from a rich uncle, including the mill at Flatford. He bought the Dedham water mill and two windmills nearer East Bergholt. Though John did work for a year learning the miller's craft, his father was an understanding parent who let his son follow his natural artistic career.

A palette and paintbox with brushes, knives and phials of pigment, which belonged to John Constable.
Constable family collection

Constable made friends through life, and for life, with people of all classes. For example, he was encouraged by Sir George Beaumont of Coleorton, whose mother lived at Dedham. He allowed Constable to borrow his favourite painting, by Claude, so that the painter could copy it. At the same time Constable was roaming the fields all about Dedham in the company of John Dunthorne, the village plumber, and amateur painter, while they studied nature and practised sketching together. In 1795 he went to London to study art, exhibiting at the Royal Academy in 1802. He was spending his summers in the country, "living nearly always in the fields and seeing nobody but field labourers." A year later he wrote, "I feel more than ever a decided conviction that I shall some time or other make some good pictures—pictures that shall be valuable to posterity if I do not reap the benefit of them."

But he was at that time a prophet in his own country; his simple, fresh style was not appreciated. Up to 1814 he did not sell a picture to anyone outside a small circle of friends, but he was sustained in adversity by the love of and by Maria Bicknell. Because her father did not consider him a suitable partner their courtship had to be carried on largely through correspondence for five years before they were able to marry, when he was forty and Maria twenty-nine. Still public success eluded him, to the degree that it was actually a Frenchman who bought "A Landscape—Noon", after it was exhibited at the Royal Academy in 1821. It was bought back eventually and now can be seen in the National Gallery under its better known title of "The Hay Wain."

Constable's wife died in 1828, leaving him with seven children, the youngest but a year old. No wonder that it has been said, "The final period, from 1828 to the year of his own death in 1837, is characterised, in general, by a sombreness of mood, tending to melancholy."* During this period there was evidence of his growing reputation; the artist himself recorded an incident in 1832: "In the coach yesterday, coming from Suffolk, were two gentlemen and myself, all strangers to each other. In passing the vale of Dedham, one of them remarked, on my saying it was beautiful, 'Yes, sir, this is Constable's country,' " That must have been very gratifying to a great artist still hoping for public recognition who had already produced masterpieces like "The Hay Wain", "The View on the Stour Near Dedham", "The Leaping Horse", "The Cornfield," and "Dedham Vale, Morning, 1811."

The last studio of the late Sir Alfred Munnings is in Dedham. This skilful painter of horses, who became President of the Royal Academy in 1944 was as fond of the Vale of Dedham as Constable. He said of Dedham, "I was in the meadow adjoining the river and on the sloping bank I lay down. Happier by far than I have been these twenty years." He resigned a controversial Presidency in December 1949, writing, "I've done. Clear. No more troubles." He died ten years later and a memorial tablet to him was placed next to that celebrating John Constable in the crypt of St Paul's Cathedral where his ashes were interred. Beneath his carved profile are the lines composed by the Poet Laureate:

"O friend how very lovely are the things
The English things, you helped us to perceive."

His studio at Castle House is kept as it was in his lifetime and is open Wednesday and Sunday afternoons in the summer season.

*A. Brooks and A. Stuart, *Constable and his Country.*

Street scene, Dedham.   *Walter A. Blythin*

The village street of Dedham presents a picturesque parade of history. The architectural writer Nikolaus Pevsner says, "Dedham is easily the most attractive small town in Essex," and, "There is nothing at Dedham to hurt the eye." People who go there may not be able to put it so succinctly, but they come away with exactly the same feeling. Outstanding of course is the church of St Mary the Virgin, built to the glory of God from the profits of the cloth industry. It was not long after its beginning in 1492 that the tide of woollen wealth was ebbing. It was completed by about 1520; 170 feet long with a 130 feet high tower at the western end. The north aisle was specially built to the memory and at the cost of the two best-known local families, the Webbs and the Gurdons. Opposite it stands Shermans, built about 1735 and now owned by the National Trust. Its early Georgian architecture in mellow brick with pilasters and pediment in stone to frame the doorway are attractive enough, but a further point of interest is the sundial high in the centre of the parapet. What has been adjudged the most important house in the place, Southfields, lies three hundred yards south of the village. It was built about 1500 as the residence, storehouse and offices of a leading clothier of the times and a member of the Sherman family.

Edmund Sherman, ancestor of General Sherman of American civil war fame was first cousin to Samuel Sherman, also of Dedham, who emigrated to Massachusetts in 1634 and settled in Contentment, which was later renamed Dedham. Edmund lies in the churchyard; his journey to the grave was short—just across the road from that house still known as Shermans. We should not leave the church itself without noting that the entire interior was restored in 1960. The six angels carved from chestnut by Aileen Kent were installed then in the sanctuary and chancel. It was here that Canon G.H.Rendall ended his days, dying in 1945 aged ninety-three. He wrote, *Dedham in history* and *Dedham Described and Deciphered*, as well as books and pamphlets to support his contention that Shakespeare was in fact Edward de Vere, seventeenth Earl of Oxford.

From Dedham it is a pleasant amble along a lane across the busy A12 to Langham, a scattered settlement with farm and church standing in companionable seclusion down the narrowest of drives, with the Hall at a distance. The latter dates from about 1740; Church Farm's timber framing is a century older, but both are striplings when compared with the age of the church which stands against a row of superb chestnut trees. Its situation suggests Saxon origin though the existing architecture is now no earlier than twelfth century. The church guide, a model of its kind, shows the devolution of the manor down the years, including the granting of it by Charles II to his druggist, Humphrey Thayer, and its ownership since 1932 by the Maturin-Baird family.

Much of the original church and some of its memorials were obscured or lost in Victorian restorations before and after the serious fire in the tower in 1879. That loss is balanced by the interesting modern work in the carved oak screens, and through all the changes the remains of the Vigerous family have lain undisturbed beneath the centre aisle ever since the last member took his eternal rest in 1629. Another local family, the Darlings, living at Langham Hall in Victorian times, is remembered in the windows of the south aisle. The six bells, including one cast by the well-known bell-founder Miles Graye in 1618, are regularly rung. In a recess in the south wall of the aisle, originally prepared for a tomb, there now stands what is claimed to be the oldest church chest in the county, made by the simple but lengthy process of hollowing out of a great baulk of oak a cavity sufficient to keep the sum of money collected for the crusade in obedience to the decree of 1166. In the churchyard a curious little building, neat in its small dimensions and graceful proportions, was erected in 1832 by the rector, Dr Hurlock, to serve as, "a girls' school on weekdays and a resting place for the poor and infirm between services on Sundays." The Trust he established to give it continuity now supports an active Sunday School in the village hall.

For all the features to be found in Langham the one over-riding tourist attraction must be that Constable strolled about these lanes and fields and found subjects worthy of his skill. Comparison between the area today and the painter's interpretation of its appearance one hundred and fifty years ago reveals the painter's felicity to his subject and the continuing beauty of the rural landscape today. Even the A12 has been routed with care to preserve this quality. Gone are the days when all the traffic had to negotiate the steep and dangerous bends on Gun Hill. Some thoughtful person had a notice in cast iron put up here which read:

"The Dumb Animals Humble Petition
Rest Drivers rest on this steep hill,
Dumb Beasts pray use with all good will.
Goad not, scourge not, with thonged whips,
Let not one curse escape your lips.
God sees and hears."

This now obsolete notice has been removed to the church porch for greater safety.

Langham cannot be left without reference to Godfreys, for though it started life as a mere gamekeeper's cottage, it became, in 1932, the home of S. L. Bensusan, whose "chronicles of rural life, which centre in the imaginary Maychester, can never be surpassed as portrayals of the traditional Essex character, now disappearing forever." They can be read in *Marshland Voices*, *Annals of Maychester*, *Marshland Calling* and other books.

At Boxted the Church of St Peter has a Norman tower consisting of "pudding stone with a generous use of mortar". The body of the church was finally finished off in brick in the early sixteenth century. Among the monuments within is one to Elizabeth, wife of Nathaniel Bacon, who died in 1628, complete with an epitaph supported by figures of an angel and a skeleton. Another epitaph perpetuates the memory of Sir Richard Blackmore who died in 1729. He was physician-in-ordinary to William III and Queen Anne and wrote much about medicine, religion and literature. His poem, "Creation" was highly praised by Dr Johnson.

The spirit of the place has been captured in modern days by paintings like "Boxted Water Meadows" on view in the Chelmsford and Essex Museum, painted by Anthony Atkinson who lives in neighbouring Great Horkesley and is head of the art department at the Colchester Technical College. The beautiful countryside dotted with picturesque old houses and farms was one reason perhaps for the increase in housing estates all the way out from Colchester to Boxted Cross. Luckily the flow has stopped there below the church and the fine brick Hall built in the early seventeenth century.

Lawford is just a mile or two up the A137 from Ardleigh. The Hall, marked in Gothic letters on the map as an antiquity worth noting, lies north of the village down a cul-de-sac signposted to the church. It is an Elizabethan mansion in timber and plaster, seen from the air to be in the form of an "E". From the ground all this is hidden by the refacing of the front in brick in the Georgian style of 1756, except, that is, for two Tudor chimneys with eight-sided shafts.

The church is remarkable in the county for its chancel built in the early fourteenth century. It is suffused with carving in which the medieval masons have given full rein to their imagination. In the tracery of thick foliage which climbs the window shafts can be seen an owl and some squirrels and when those craftsmen came to fashion the easternmost window on the north side they conjured from the stone two ribbons of little men, tumbling, dancing, making music; happiness in religion personified. The rest of the church still dates from just a little later in the same century, though the tower has been much repaired with brickwork. There is an interesting Victorian addition in the east window and reredos beneath, which was carved from alabaster by C. F. Hayward in 1884 in keeping, it was probably thought at the time, with the medieval elaboration. The Waldegrave monument of 1584 reminds us that this family was at the Hall into the seventeenth century, when Jemima Waldegrave was courted by Simon D'Ewes the diarist.

Manningtree was quite a port in the days when the river Stour, on which it stands, was navigable all the way up to Sudbury. Those were prosperous days, but railway and road successively made waterborne carriage slow and uneconomic. The little market town carried on in the same quiet way that might be expected of a community which, as the headquarters of the Manni tribe, greeted Caesar when he came to reconnoitre in 55 B.C. In recent years it has had to undergo a further change in function and form. Older houses have fallen into decay; business changes have brought demolition and rebuilding, but still the cross formed by High Street and South Street shows interesting Georgian architecture. The church of St Michael and All Angels has roof, a wall and windows built in 1616, but the remainder dates from the restoration of 1839.

This place will always be famous as the burial-place of Matthew Hopkins in 1647. In an age of superstition and religious fervour he obtained a commission from Parliament to go on a witch-hunting circuit for three years. Essex had already achieved a reputation for the number of its witches, their trials and executions. Hopkins was pleased to assume the title of "Witchfinder General". He was allowed twenty shillings for every town he visited and formed his own team of men to comb the Tendring area, moving on to St Osyth and thence into Suffolk, Norfolk and Huntingdonshire. Soon he had thirty-two people under arrest of whom nineteen were hanged in one day. He worked up to a peak of two hundred in jail and sixty-eight hanged. He used all manner of torture to wring false confessions out of bewildered, ignorant countrywomen. Eventually the shame of the proceedings reached the ears of Parliament and Hopkins found it necessary to publish a pamphlet in his own defence in 1647. A commission inquired into his methods and condemned them, although it did not see evil in the witch-hunt itself. Hopkins retired discreetly to Manningtree where he died later the same year blameless and unpunished because people still believed that such poor old crones and gaffers were witches.

CHAPTER SIX

From the Stour Around the Coast to the Colne and Wivenhoe

MISTLEY, in the Tendring District, is a large industrialised village on the Stour estuary adjoining Manningtree. By Mistley railway station the B1352 bears away inland from the Malthouses towards New Mistley. It was the old village which thrived on the river trade, owing its development to Richard Rigby, one of the few financiers actually to make a fortune from the notorious South Sea Bubble, who rebuilt Mistley Hall before his death in 1730. That Hall has been demolished but its two lodges, designed by Robert Adam, still exist away to the west where the B1035 approaches Manningtree. Rigby saw that here at Mistley was the site for a centre of trade. He laid out the quayside and built the tall malthouses purely for business reasons; now visitors say that they add "character".

Though old and new have now merged together, New Mistley was in fact the brain child of Rigby's son, also named Richard, who, in the last quarter of the eighteenth century, aimed at making Mistley a spa where the richer folk might take the waters or simply stroll around the little square where a swan stands in the circular basin of a charming fountain. That stroll and that fountain can still be enjoyed today. Robert Adam was asked to submit plans for the development, and they were actually used for the building of two towers in 1776 at either end of the nave of a church put up in 1735. The nave grew old and unsafe and was demolished, the same fate nearly befell the towers, but their worth was recognized and they were placed in the care of the Department of the Environment so that they can be seen and enjoyed by the country as a whole.

Bradfield, the next village, has its Hall on a moated site a mile or so south of church and inn past the newer, larger settlement of Bradfield Heath. The Hall looks plain enough from the road but at the back there is a lovely gable in red brick patterned with blue, and windows which recall an early Tudor building—the place in which Sir Harbottle Grimston was born in 1603. The Grimstons had bought the place from the Waldegraves about thirty years previously and Harbottle grew up there to become M.P. for Harwich in 1628 and for Colchester in 1640. He played a great part in the negotiations with Charles I when he was on the Isle of Wight and for his pains was sent to the Tower until the King was executed; but his true worth was recognized in 1660 when he was made speaker of the House of Commons and was asked to welcome Charles II to England and the throne. The seven hundred year old church of St Lawrence stands yet, though its exterior has all been covered with nineteenth century stucco in a well-meaning restoration.

Continuing along the B1352 there are glimpses across the Stour and a closer look when one turns down the lane to Wrabness—Wrabbs promontory, a sight for sore eyes when Saxon seamen made their landfall and pulled their boats up on the bank to settle here and make their leader's name ring through the centuries. The railway station makes a nucleus of the new Wrabness; the Hall and the Church are found in the loop of road which heads under the railway towards the Stour and returns over it west of the station. The church is of interest because it is not the proud possessor of a spire or tower. Its bell hangs in a "cage" built separately in the churchyard, just a mere clapboard shed made more notable by its age and by its unusualness in Essex.

From the station the lane climbs Primrose Hill to the B1352 which skirts Stour Wood on its way to Ramsey. As a village it just manages to preserve its identity at the junction with the A604, but after the church has been passed on the main road the build-up to the port begins. The parish actually stretches across the horn of land that is Harwich, so, as well as having a good length of riverside scenery, it can also boast that it has one foot, albeit small and marshy, in the North Sea.The village's greatest landmark must be its mill, built in 1842, and now, as a post mill, a rare feature in the county. It was still working after the last war. The church in its fabric and furniture runs through five centuries in a variety of styles from a twelfth century window to an Elizabethan pulpit with remarkable panelling.

The former Tendring Rural District guide says, "In contrast to the rural charm of Ramsey village, three miles away by road but within the same parish, is the work-a-day bustle of Parkeston, which now accounts for the major part of Ramsey parish's population of 2,300." Its history as a rail-boat connection with the continent dates from 15th February 1883 when the Great Eastern Railway transferred its continental service from the pier at Harwich to the railhead and quay built on reclaimed land and called Parkeston after Charles Henry Parker who was then Chairman of the railway company. The quay now extends to three thousand feet of berths, warehouses and railway sidings and ferries sail twice a day.

Harwich had been a port and a harbour long before new-fangled things like railways were ever thought of and it prospers still with ferries to Europe and Scandinavia for goods and travellers. What is more it later recaptured a great deal of rail trade with its roll-on, roll-off rail ferry terminal, a big industrial bonus for a town of some fifteen thousand people. It lives too, on the ancillary services which a harbour needs, like the Trinity House vessels which work out from Harwich on the many navigational aids required around the coast and in the busy sea lanes. The visitor can simply stand on the sidelines, observing all the harbour activity or take the ferry to Felixstowe or Parkeston.

One architectural expert has stated "Although present-day Harwich might well be called the poor relation of Dovercourt, it is pleasant to look at and to wander in . . . " Unusual items of interest include the Town Hall, built in 1864—as the *Great Eastern Hotel!*— a five-storeyed fancy in white brick; there are still two other inns nearby to satisfy the sailors' thirst, the *Pier Hotel* and the *Angel Inn*. From the pierhead one can stroll southwards, noting Georgian facades in West Street and Church Street, where the *Three Cups Hotel* shows its four hundred years existence in the plaster ceiling on the first floor, which Drake and Nelson would both have seen when they were being

Pilot house, Harwich *Owen Keen*

High Lighthouse, Harwich *Owen Keen*

shown to their rooms, though only the latter would have seen the Guildhall opposite for it was not built until 1769. Carry on past the church and you will come to the "umbrella" lighthouse on the Green and beyond it the "high" lighthouse, both of which were built in 1818 to replace older lights, and now they are themselves superseded. Go on a little further to see on that same green, which was once the shipyard, the wooden crane, operated by a treadmill in its weatherboarded house, which dates from the last half of the seventeenth century and is claimed to be unique in the world. Back along the wall is the quay where local boats land their catches of fish from the North Sea. At the Navyard Wharf there is great bustle and business in the loading of cars and containers for shipping to countries such as Scandinavia and the United States. A local guide indicates other pleasant walks, upstream along the Stour or round the point of Beacon Hill which divides Harwich and Dovercourt. Defoe summed up Harwich in 1724 as " . . . a town of hurry and business not much of gaiety and pleasure, yet the inhabitants seem warm in their nests and some of them very wealthy." Leonard Weaver has used this quotation on the title page of his *The Harwich Story* which is a fascinating account of the place from the prehistoric, represented by the dug-out canoe found in the harbour, right down to the reorganization of local government in 1974 which made the Borough part of the new Tendring District Council and turned the Town Hall into the offices for the Chief Technical Officer.

Dovercourt Front   *Owen Keen*

Dovercourt is a popular place for people to retire to; one London Borough has had bungalows built here in its bracing air to give their senior citizens a really restful old age. One of the sights those older Londoners enjoy is the crowds of younger people, parents and children, having a happy holiday, for Dovercourt has a lot to offer. As a seaside town it is new, for it was only around 1850 that the little village on the main road was extended seaward as a resort, largely the idea of Mr John Bagshaw, Harwich's Member of Parliament. All the same it can be said that Dovercourt is mentioned in the Domesday Book and Harwich was not settled at that time. It was under the Duke of Norfolk's Lordship of the Manor of Harwich at the beginning of the thirteenth century that the place began to develop. It became a great base for Britain's Navy, and shipbuilding continued into this century though the Royal Dockyard was transferred to Sheerness in 1677. Just before that date Anthony Deane, later knighted and friend of Samuel Pepys, secured the position of Master Shipwright at Harwich and superintended the building of eight ships to challenge a strong Dutch navy.

After the holiday camp below Dovercourt the foreshore gets marshy and there is not a road, and hardly a footpath to give access to the marshes and saltings which are intersected by Oakley Creek, Hamford Water, Kirby Creek and Walton Channel to form Pewit, Skipper, Horsey and Hedge-end Islands. Then the Naze stands out starkly like a bulwark guarding Walton. From the sea the most prominent landmark is the tall thin brick tower standing on the highest point. It is known as the Naze Tower and was built in 1720, probably replacing an earlier construction, by Trinity House to serve as a beacon to shipping.

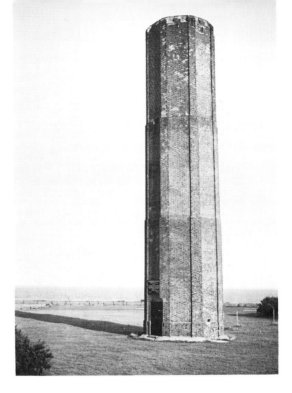

Trinity House tower at the Naze, Walton.

Walter A. Blythin

The sea has always been an enemy of Walton, undermining the cliffs and claiming so much land that it is said that the ruins of the old village of Walton have been found on the West Rocks, some nine miles out in the North Sea. The original church was swallowed up by the waves in 1798. The nearly half mile long pier for many years ranked next to Southend as the longest pier in the kingdom, and it has a railway with, at the pierhead, the lifeboat station. Here one has a good view of ships into and out from Harwich and passing coasters with at night the "amusements", all lit up, adding to the holiday atmosphere.

Walton is almost surrounded by water, for the Walton Channel creeps in behind the town to provide acres of safe water and calm saltings. Just the right situation for a boating lake where sailing, rowing and paddle boats can be hired while the more expert gather in the Frinton and Walton Yacht Club whose clubhouse is adjacent. Nearby is the Martello Tower and beyond a generous caravan park. A walk back towards the pier will take in the patches of earth called by geologists Red Crag, which are so rich in fossils, particularly of shells. Where that shelly sand spills from the cliff and across the shore you will invariably see the fossil-hunter.

The present town of Walton originates from the start of the fashion for sea bathing as a novel and health-giving pastime. Barker's *Marine Hotel*, though now much altered and modernised, was one of the first buildings put up, around 1825. Marine Parade, then called The Crescent, was built in 1832 as the first complete street. Soon afterwards John Warner, a bellfounder from Hoddesdon, invested in the building of a terrace on the Cliff, including East Cliff Cottage, with its pretty bargeboarding, which he had built especially for his mother. It is known today as the Gothic cottage.

65

Frinton and Walton are like an old married couple—they have been together so long that they have lost their separate identity. It was not so very long ago, about ninety years in fact, that Frinton was merely a fishing village. Then came that Victorian seaside boom, and Sir Richard Cooker saw that the breezy air on the cliff-top, the health-giving ozone straight off the sea would be a great attraction to holiday makers. So up went the houses in tree-lined avenues which are still good examples of town planning. The elegance of Victorian and Edwardian houses, standing in their own grounds is varied now with smaller houses, a good shopping centre and the inevitable tower block where flats have replaced some of the unmanageable old houses and hotels.

All the usual seaside amenities are here for those seeking a quiet uncommercialised holiday. There is no pier, there are no shops on the promenade, and a byelaw prohibits the loud playing of transistor radios. Instead of the usual run of amusement arcades and bingo halls there is a long, grassy verge which runs all along the cliff top, and is even marked on the Ordnance Survey maps as The Greensward. From it one can descend through cliff gardens to the sea wall and the beach which is washed clean by every tide. It was planned like this as long ago as 1903 when the Frinton Sea Defences Act allowed the expenditure of no less than £32,000 on forming a massive sea wall and promenade behind thirty-two breakwaters which serve to trap the sun and temper the breeze.

The only place left which has a connection with the former village is the church of Old St Mary's, as distinguished from New St Mary's built in Old Road in 1929, which claims Tudor origin in its brick porch though its nave and chancel are a restoration of 1879. The great storm of 1703 had blown down most of the church, reducing its usable part so much that it could for many years be claimed to be the smallest church in the kingdom.

Frinton finishes on the golf course. Motorists can get no further than the car park outside the nineteenth hole. Holland-on-Sea was once a small village called Little Holland, isolated and inundated countless times. Now it is tranformed, set out in regular little rows of houses and bungalows, very much the older people's end of Clacton, just as Butlin's Holiday Camp and all the fun of the fair appeals to the younger element on the southern side. In between can be seen miles of sandy shore backed by what the British Motor Corporation's guide described as an "Exceedingly attractive, up-to-date seaside health and holiday resort, characterized by charming modern houses, good shops, and wide roadways and noted for dry and sunny climate and tonic air."

It is indeed a pleasant and very popular resort with excellent road and rail connections to London and beyond. There is a vast influx of visitors in the season but the entertainment and facilities are on a scale to cope with it. The pier and promenade offer shows featuring top-flight entertainers and many other attractions. In 1966 Mr Kenneth Walker wrote a history of Clacton, commissioned by the Council as a permanent record of the town: the story of an ancient maritime village, the home of bishops and smugglers, and the story of the modern seaside resort. Mr Walker takes us back to the early Stone Age people who, in the fashioning of flint implements found here in great numbers, gave the archaeological world the Clactonian Industry as an historical milestone. Thousands of years later a New Stone

Age tribe lived at Jaywick, producing a distinctive kind of decorated pottery now known as Rinyo-Clacton, so the town's name is twice over noised abroad in archaeological circles.

Great Clacton was first settled inland by the Celts. At Bull Hill, now an industrial area, they had set up their own industry in the making of pots. Roman remains are scanty, but there is no denying they were here to add a chapter to the story which is continued by the Saxons, when one tribal leader named Clacc brought his "ing" or people over the sea to create this community or "ton". So "Clacc-ing-ton" slipped into the English language and was soon shortened by the natives to its present form.

At the coming of the Conqueror all the land hereabouts was vested in the Bishop of London whose house stood somewhere near St John's Church and whose appurtenances included a huge fishpond and a vineyard near the present Valley Road. In the sixteenth century Thomas Darcy, cousin to Queen Jane Seymour, and created Baron Darcy of Chich, the former name of St Osyth, was able to obtain the lands of the manors of St Osyth, Great and Little Clacton and Weeley from the royal family for the sum of £3,974. 9s. 4½d. and his descendants enjoyed the inheritance through three hundred years. A Victorian who added a certain spice to Clacton life was Dr Thomas Harding Newman, who lived at Eaglehurst in Valley Road. He was quite eccentric; one of the many practical jokes he played on local people was a visit he made one day to London wearing a brown wig—returning the following morning ostentatiously sporting a grey wig; thereby convincing Clactonians that his experiences in the wicked capital had turned his hair grey overnight!

From Mr. Walker's excellent account, a paragraph will serve to sum up: "Although the ancient village of Great Clacton is now absorbed into the modern town there still lingers about it the atmosphere of its former independence, and its older buildings and mellow roofs remind one that this was the centre of local life for centuries before Clacton-on-Sea ever appeared on the map. One by one, however, its little cottages are giving way to flats and houses, and others acquire a new look, but its Norman church and its delightful old inns should long remain as witnesses to a past age."

Tendring is the village central to the area, although the old Rural District offices were at Weeley. The new, larger Tendring District Council, which includes Harwich, Walton, Frinton, Clacton and Brightlingsea operates from Clacton. The village offers at least three points of interest. The church not only for its age—thirteenth century nave and chancel, fourteenth century timber porch—but also for one unusual feature, a single hammerbeam roof truss above the two doorways with tracery carving which makes it contemporary with the porch and therefore earlier than the famed hammerbeam roof of Westminster Hall. A second point of interest is the splendid holly hedge on either side of the village street; and the third is the old union workhouse, now known as Heath Hospital.

It was in this place that the well-known Kitty Canham was born in 1720 to Robert Canham, a farmer at Beaumont Hall. Kitty caused quite a sensation when sometime after marrying Mr Gough the worthy vicar of Thorpe-le-Soken, she merely walked out, and no one saw her go. Her poor husband had a terrible shock later, when he heard her mentioned as a viscountess.

The church of St Edmund, Tendring.

Walter A. Blythin

Kitty left Essex and, at some time, met Lord Dalmeny, son of the second Earl of Rosebery. He fell in love with her, and Kitty married her Lord without telling him that she was already the partner of a village priest. They then embarked upon a whirlwind of travel, until, in 1752, at Verona, Kitty fell ill, and died. It is said that, on her deathbed, she wrote her confession: "I am the wife of the Reverend Alexander Gough, Vicar of Thorpe-le-Soken, in Essex. My maiden name was Catherine Canham. My last request is to be buried at Thorpe." Despite the difficulties, Lord Dalmeny went to tremendous trouble to have the body of his bride of such brief acquaintance embalmed and transported by land and sea to meet her last request, without giving away her shameful secret. Off the English coast the ship was boarded by Customs officers looking for contraband. They insisted on opening the chest in which poor Kitty lay, and received such a shock that it required explanation, and so the secret was exposed, but I am pleased to report that, at the interment at Thorpe-le-Soken, the two men in her life stood side by side to pay their last respects.

Thorpe-le-Soken has another celebrity in Sir William Withey Gull who was born at Colchester on 31st December 1816, the youngest son of John Gull, barge owner and wharfinger who lived in this village. In 1856 William, having studied medicine, was appointed a "full" physician at Guy's Hospital. He attended the Prince of Wales when he contracted typhoid fever in 1871 and brought him successfully back to health.

68

He also received royal favour as a reward and was created physician in ordinary to the Queen in 1882. He died of a third heart attack on 29th January 1890. His talent for teaching was extraordinary, and his powers of public speaking made him a very impressive lecturer. He was aided by a power of physical endurance which allowed him to see one patient after another over a long period with the closest concentration being given to each individual. His success can be judged from a temporal point of view by the £344,000 fortune he amassed excluding his landed estates.

There is however, a very sinister rumour abroad in the village that Sir William's body was never buried; that the coffin which was lowered into the grave was filled with stones to give it weight, and Sir William Gull, alias Jack the Ripper, was locked away in a private madhouse to bring to an end the series of horrific butcherings of London prostitutes. But until the grave is opened up a rumour it must remain.

The church stands behind the houses on the main street, and was rebuilt just a hundred years ago. Its original establishment was way back in Saxon times and the strong west tower of Tudor brick is a stepping stone in its stream of history. Another small clue to its antiquity is the base of the present font which has been dated to 1147, while the pretty weathervane which crowns the spire was put up in 1902. At the west end of the village a good-sized Georgian house called Comarques was once lived in by Arnold Bennett.

Kirby-le-Soken lies due east on the B1034. The church of St Michael reflects a very thorough restoration by architect Henry Stone just on a hundred years ago. In its registers, which go back to 1681, one can see in the burials how the vicar received as a fee the "best upper garment" of the deceased. A strange custom of these ancient Sokens which here was honoured up to 1707.

Weeley is a village south of Tendring, but central enough to house the old Rural District Council Headquarters. A triangle of roads, including the A133 and B1033 forms a nucleus of houses old and new, close to the railway station which gives many town workers a chance to live in the country. The church now stands quite isolated where the old Hall once kept it company up a track off the main road. Since it is not a hundred years old it can be said to be a modern restoration, though its records (which go back to 1562) show that, back in the days when Napoleon threatened to invade England, extensive barracks were built on the heath which then reached right up to the church and many a marriage between gallant soldier and country maid is entered on those parchment pages to be followed, just after the turn of the century, by the baptisms of the children of those wartime marriages.

West of Weeley is the parish of Great Bentley. It could be called a scattered settlement simply because its village green, all 42 acres of it, is the largest clear green in England. That means quite a walk from one side to the other, but the vicar has to do it every day since vicarage and church are on opposite sides. The green is well kept and includes a cricket pitch. When a match is in progress it is hard to appreciate the scene on this spot when Rose Allin, a martyr to her religious beliefs, was brought out of prison in Colchester Castle to be burnt at the stake on her village green.

From here a lane runs west to join the B1029 in Thorrington where the person to note is not an historical character but a modern benefactor. The late John Girling gave several acres of land in the centre of the village to form a playing field. Almost five hundred years before him another benefactor, John Deth, supplied the money for the building of the tower of St Mary's Church, which was so smoothly built of knapped flint that it has been described by a famous architect as a "cobble pavement put up vertically." Today the church is relatively isolated from the village, with only the Hall for company, but it is worth visiting for, among other interesting features, it is claimed to have one of the most beautiful churchyards in the county.

Brightlingsea is due south, and the name comes from Brihtling, a Saxon who once ruled in this area. Cindery Island, the sandbank in the Brightlingsea Creek, derives from the Old English for "low-lying land". These names point to the early settlement of the place and the importance from those early days of Brightlingsea as a port at the mouth of the Colne River. The whole town was once an island and is shown as such on a sixteenth century map. Today the ancient port is delineated by an arrowhead of land washed by the Alresford Creek on the north, the Colne River to the west and the Brightlingsea and Flag Creeks to the south.

Its complete history up to the last war has been written in fascinating detail by E. P. Dickin, who starts from the earliest times: "Brightlingsea had many attractions for early man . . . a landlocked island, two good harbours, plenty of water, good supplies of fish, oysters and other shellfish, good landing places and easy communication with the mainland were great advantages. We may be sure this desirable residence was soon occupied." That the occupation continued is shown by the Roman remains which have turned up from time to time. Workmen laying water pipes back in 1884 had to hack their way through the beautiful mosaic pavement of a Roman villa; another fine dwelling of that age stood by the old railway track just east of Alfresford Creek. Its remains were discovered by Australian troops in camp there on a trench-digging exercise during the First World War. Many a fisherman has dredged up Roman remains from the sea bed of the old port, including a splendid urn brought up in 1871 and now in the Colchester and Essex Museum.

"Ships and men who sail them have always played an important part in the history of Brightlingsea. It is likely that the ferryman who takes you on the short trip across the creek to St Osyth Stone has seen strange sights in strange lands, because it is said that wherever a river joins the sea, there you will find a Brightlingsea man". So says the local guide and proof of this contention is visible in very striking form in the parish church of All Saints, where there is a frieze of tiles all round the church, each of which records the details of Brightlingsea men lost in disasters at sea all over the world from 1872 onwards. There are more than two hundred of these unusual little memorials. Their originator is disclosed on the very first tile: "This record commences from the time when Arthur Pertwee became vicar of this parish"; and the second tile records the loss of David Day, with his schooner, the *William* of Hartlepool on 9th December 1872, aged forty-nine. The last tile to complete the circle of the walls comes ninety years later in August 1962 when a man was lost off the yacht *Sammy*.

This church, now well over a mile from the centre of population, is replaced by a chapel-of-ease, built in 1837 and dedicated to St James, where the church keeps company with the shops, post office and Town Hall. But the old church has not been forgotten and has recently been restored by a sympathetic band of "Friends", maintaining its links with the past. Nicholas Magens, who made a mint of money from insurance up to his death in 1764, for instance, made arrangements in advance

Robert Aldous, with foreman Rashbrook, making the daily round of his Brightlingsea yard.   *John Leather* to lay out £6,000 on a magnificent, if showy, memorial in the chancel as a symbol of his earthly success. Another family closely connected with All Saints is the Beriffes who have seven brasses commemorating their passing between 1496 and 1578. Much of the original church was built with their money, for they were rich merchants, and their special mark is incorporated in it. John, first man to die, made every effort to perpetuate the family name; by three wives he had nineteen children, thirteen of them sons, all of them growing up in the house called "Jacobes" in the High Street, which having been recorded as early as 1315, rates seven lines in Pevsner's book on the buildings of Essex, which is quite an honour. It still adds grace and interest to the street scene.

The newer church supports the town clock celebrating Queen Victoria's Golden Jubilee. A local man told me that Brightlingsea is noted for the large number of elderly people who have chosen the place for their retirement. Because there is no through road the town has been able to preserve its peaceful and spacious seaside charm. It also keeps alive its connection with the Cinque Port of Sandwich by choosing a Deputy who declares an oath of allegiance to the Mayor of Sandwich and makes a token payment of fifty pence to represent the ships and men it places at the disposal of the Cinque Port. The Mayor then invests the Deputy with the badge and chain of office, a superb opal, said to be one of the biggest in the world, carved in the form of a seascape, which is attached to a chain made of alternate links of oyster shells and crossed sprats carried out in solid silver. It was presented to the town by Mr John Bateman in 1893 after this interesting ceremony, stated in 1442 to have existed "from time immemorial" was happily revived in 1888. Every year since, on the Monday after St Andrew's day, "Choosing the Deputy" is re-enacted in the belfry of the hundred-feet high tower of All Saints Church. Brightlingsea had its glamour days in the Victorian age of steam yachts and international racing of sailing boats. It was an eccentric American millionaire, Bayard Brown, living on his yacht in the harbour, who gave the town its recreation ground and the fine peal of tubular bells in the old church. The first yacht of that era to be built in the local shipyard in 1846 was the 10-ton *Fawn* for J. R. Kirby, a product of the Aldous yard of recent memory.

But things and people change and Brightlingsea has had to forget its glamour and continue earning its living from a much wider crowd of boating enthusiasts. The Aldous yard has now been bought up by the local authority to be leased to small industries which make their contribution not only to the yachting industry but also to the life of the town itself.

Visitors from all over the world make their way to St Osyth, a village reached from Brightlingsea by the ferry across the Creek or, for motorists, by the B1027 from Colchester. This is not the name it was given by the first settlers in Saxon times; they called it "the bend in the creek"—the characteristic which made it a defensible place, and soon it was shortened to "bend" or, in their language "Chich" and that is what it was entered under in the Domesday Book. The great change in Saxon lives came with the spread of Christianity through the Anglo-Saxon tribes in this new country. Frithewald, King of the East Angles, became the first Christian ruler of that tribe. He had married Wilburga, daughter of Penda, Saxon King of Mercia, today's Midlands, and they had a daughter who was dear to them. They called her Osyth, or Osgith as it was better known in those days. The rough life of the settlement, with constant risk of attack by Danes or Vikings was not suitable for the daughter of a king, so she was sent away to be brought up at peaceful Pollesworth in Warwickshire, under the educational influence of St Modwen, Abbess of the great religious house built there. Her Abbess sent her to fetch a book from St Edith, sister of King Alfred. Since this was long before the invention of printing every book had to be handwritten; such a laborious task that every book was a treasure in itself, and the carrying of one a trustworthy task. On the way back she had to cross a river in dreadful weather. The wind was so strong that it plucked her from the bridge into the flooding stream. The old story tells that when the Abbess found she had not returned at the expected time she went looking for her. After searching unsuccessfully for three days she met St Edith, who did not know Osyth was missing but had been told by an angel in a vision to go to that very river. So the two good women knelt down and prayed together that they might find Osyth, little realising that she had been drowned at that very spot. At the end of their prayers St Edith called "Osyth, Osyth, Osyth!" in a loud voice, and to their surprise the lost girl was seen rising from the waters, miraculously restored to life and bearing quite undamaged that precious book.

Though today that incident hardly seems likely it probably was based on some incident in Osyth's life at the Abbey which, after a thousand years' telling and retelling, has been altered out of recognition. After such a scare her parents would be glad when she was able to return home as a grown woman, and just as they had made a happy marriage they hoped their daughter would do the same. To this end they made arrangements, as was the fashion in those days, for her to be betrothed to Sighere, King of the East Saxons, Essex as we know it today. Osyth was unhappy because she had hoped to continue her life of prayer and service in a convent, but her parents must be obeyed.

On the wedding day there were great celebrations, and Sighere laughed and joked with his trusty chiefs. A great white stag came out of the forest and almost up to the doors of the palace and the King could not resist the call to the hunt. Off he went in a bustle and a clatter, leaving Osyth to the care of the womenfolk. This gave the girl the opportunity she needed. She slipped away to a nearby convent and "took the veil". Sighere ought to have been very put out when he came back, tired and hungry from the hunt to find that his betrothed had fled, but apparently his love for her was such that he forgave her. Knowing that she could not go back on her holy vows, he demonstrated that love by settling on her his village of Chich that she might build a nunnery there and form her own community. All seemed happiness now for Osyth whose piety and knowledge inspired the women about her as they prayed together and cared for the poor and the sick. But in the eastern corner of Essex times were troubled still, as those northern invaders brought death and destruction to the Anglo-Saxon settlements.

St Osyth Priory.   *Owen Keen*

One autumn day in 653 a band of Danish pirates led by Inguar and Hubba came up the creek and landed near Chich. They scoured the countryside, looking for loot and laying waste all about them in their barbarian fashion. So they came to the little convent and taunted the frightened women, calling on them to give up their religion and worship the raiders' pagan gods. Despite their threats Osyth, as leader of these weak but wonderful women, refused to bow her knee to their idols. So enraged did the Danish chief become at her intransigence that he ordered her head to be cut off and a pirate leapt to do his bidding. So Osyth died for her faith, but that is not the end of the story, for legend has it that Osyth there and then stooped and picked up her head and carried it to the church she had built near her nunnery, where she struck the door with a blood-stained hand and fell dead at last. The raiders must have fled in awe of this heavenly sign that the Abbess Osyth should be buried in her church, for the nuns were able to retrieve her body and have it buried in reverence and in sorrow in the choir of that church.

73

Meanwhile, from the moment when she was beheaded and on the very spot the cruel deed was done a fountain of the clearest water gushed forth and continues to this day, in the copse still known as Nun's Wood. At the shrine of St Osyth many miracles are said to have been performed, attracting pilgrims from all parts of the country. Cures affected by her intercession were chiefly in the healing of paralysis and like ailments against which the medical skill of the time was helpless. But there was one occasion when punishment not cure was miraculously meted out. In the year 1044 Alfred, Bishop of London, tried to open St Osyth's tomb to add one of her bones to his collection of saintly relics and was straightway affected with leprosy for such heresy.

That ancient nunnery and the little church disappeared many years ago but the present church stands on the same holy site. St Osyth lived on for centuries in the memory of local folk: when people went to bed they would rake the sign of the cross in the ashes of their fire and pray to St Osyth to deliver them from fire and water, meaning floods, of course, and from all misadventure through the night to come. It is said that, once a year on her saint's day, 7th August, St Osyth comes back to the scene of her martyrdom and walks again from wood to church, carrying her head in her arms.

To cross the Colne and get access to Mersea Island it is necessary to journey back to Colchester and pass through the outskirts of Wivenhoe, where John Constable painted the cattle grazing in the fresh green pasture by the lake, with the house, built in 1761, in the distance. Wivenhoe Park was originally built for Colonel Isaac Rebow; it was General Francis Slater, who married his heiress and adopted the family name in 1796, who had the painting done in 1816, which can now been seen in the National Gallery of Art in Washington, D.C.

The General was succeeded by his son-in-law John Gurdon (he added Rebow) who had Thomas Hopper alter the house with an imitation-Tudor facade in 1853. In 1902 it was purchased for the Gooch family and remained in their ownership until in 1962 it was bought by Essex County Council as the site for the University of Essex. Now that park is covered by the low buildings of the central block and the tall, dark, brooding towers of the residential blocks. The university began operating in 1964 and achieved something of a reputation for revolt and unrest before settling down to serious work. The facilities are excellent, offering rich cultural, artistic and sociological experience to those lecturers and undergraduates who can recognise their good fortune and reap its benefits.

The village proper is much further down the B1028, where the church and the Garrison House, with its curious and beautiful pargeting—decorative plaster-work—combine with the quayside itself to make a number of picturesque views. It once served as the port of Colchester. The event which shook Wivenhoe to its foundations, literally, was the earthquake which in 1884 damaged the church very badly and wrecked houses along the quay. Quayside Cottage bears the date in its back wall which had to be rebuilt. "All in all it is a place for a restful stay, where sky and land and water meet, making views which have inspired the brushes of gifted painters and humble amateur alike."*

*S. Jarvis and C. Harrison, *In Search of Essex*

CHAPTER SEVEN

Maldon and its Hinterland

THE western bank of the Colne, and more particularly the village of Rowhedge has been delightfully described by Margaret Leather in *Saltwater Village*, a first-hand account of life in this maritime community during its late Victorian and early twentieth century heyday.

Below it is Fingringhoe, which had its share of damage in the earthquake of 1884. It was the restoration of the church after that event which led to the discovery of a faint early mural painting which is unusual for its extent. St Andrew's makes a pretty view, or, as Pevsner puts it, "Visually quite exceptionally successful, owing to its position, the view to the east, and the little pond with oak trees below to the west." The man who conducted services here through thirty-seven years up to 1959, when he died, was Gerald Montague Benton. In his spare time he delved into the history of the county, and by his scholarship and his passion for accuracy set an example to followers in this field. His life in Essex from 1922 was dedicated to work for the Essex Archaeological Society of which he was Secretary up to 1950 and President for the next five years. As Honorary Editor for many years he applied his high standards to the production of its *Transactions*.

It is interesting to learn that this little village figures in a story concerning King Edward I (1272-1307). He was here at Fingringhoe for a deer hunt when he recognized, amongst a crowd of onlookers, one of his washerwomen, called Matilda of Waltham. He teased her, betting one of his fastest horses against her joining the hunt and being in at the kill. Matilda was game, she took up the challenge, stayed the course, and collected the reward, which the king had to redeem with forty good English shillings.

Below the village, but above the marshes given over to the Fingringhoe firing ranges adjoining the river, is a nature reserve, open to the public, one of thirty-six run by the Essex Naturalists Trust, based on Fingringhoe Wick, which is their new administrative centre. Nearby is the site of a Roman fort, built to protect the river approach to Colchester.

Mersea Island is beyond the marshes and creeks which have to be skirted by the road through Abberton and Langenhoe where the church was ruined by that earthquake and rebuilt in 1886. The only road to the island, the B1025, crosses via the Strood which refers to the "marshy land" on either side rather than the road itself which is claimed to be of Roman construction. It forks left to East and right to West Mersea. Eastwards the road peters out by Ivy Hall and well before the beach at Mersea Stone; incorporated with this end of the island is a country park. In the rectory for ten years up to 1881 lived the Reverend Sabine Baring-Gould, who died aged ninety in 1924. He was a prolific author, as well as father of fifteen children, but his books would not suit modern tastes. One of them, *Mehala*, weaves melodrama and local legend into a tale which has just about the unhappiest ending I have ever read, and it all centres on the marshes and creeks and the ordinary folk who made up his parish.

West Mersea is a holiday resort in miniature. The bathing is better here and the Strood sees traffic at a standstill sometimes in the summer as the car parks get crowded. The church of St Peter and St Paul is the nucleus of the old village. Its tower is partly of early Norman construction, but the Romans had been here long before those builders, and at some time in the first century had raised a huge burial mound twenty two and a half feet high and a hundred feet in diameter. The archaeologists were puzzled when all their digging yielded only a small hole, a cube of about eighteen inches lined with Roman tiles, within which there was a casket containing a glass bowl which in turn held the cremated remains of an adult. Truly a mystery within an enigma which can never be solved. In the garden of a house in Beach Road, behind the church, can be seen the remains of another Roman burial, a wheel tomb in which a small central room has walls radiating from it to an outer wall some sixty-five feet in diameter. As early in 1730 a fine mosaic pavement of the same period was discovered to extend under West Mersea Hall and the adjoining churchyard. In fact it was found that many corpses had been buried on this pavement because the sexton could not get his shovel through it.

There is no doubt that this island had a powerful place in the Roman occupation of England. Morant, our first historian, thinks the Counts of the Saxon Shore had their headquarters here; other theories are that these are the remains of a great temple to the virgin goddess Vesta, custodian of the sacred flame, and that they are either the villa of a Roman noble or the foundations of a lighthouse or watchtower.

West of Mersea lie the Wigboroughs, Great and Little, where, again, the churches had to be largely rebuilt after the earthquake. Old inhabitants remember the night in 1916 when a Zeppelin was forced to land in a field. The crew set it on fire before marching in good order along the country lanes looking for someone to whom they could surrender. When they came up to the village constable he nearly fell off his bicycle with surprise. The farmer who owned the field charged a fee to sightseers and used the money to provide comforts for our own soldiers. Pieces of the burnt-out wreck found their way into homes all over the county, into the museums and even into the church of St Stephen adjacent to Moulsham Hall to the north.

Tollesbury a hundred years ago was a large, busy fishing village when, "A large number of the inhabitants are now engaged in culling and nursing that luscious dainty, the oyster."* The waterside is half a mile or so down the lane from the village proper to Woodrolfe Creek and the Tollesbury Fleet. Here the tall sailmaker's lofts, in tarred clapboard, loom over the mud flats where knowledge of the channels is vital to any trip out into the estuary of the Blackwater.

The square which forms the centre of town is overlooked by the squat Norman tower of the church of St Mary. An inscription round the bowl of the eighteenth century octagonal font reads, "Good people all I pray take care, That in ye church you do not sware, As this man did." For an explanation we must turn to the register

*D. W. Coller, *The People's History of Essex*

The German Zeppelin, L33, which crashed at Little Wigborough in 1916.   *John Leather*

of baptisms under 30th August, 1718: "Elizabeth, daughter of Robert and Eliza Wood, being ye first childe whom was baptized in the New Font which was bought out of five pounds paid by John Norman, who some months before came drunk into the church and cursed and talked loud in the time of Divine service, to prevent his being prosecuted for which he paid by agreement the above said five pounds. Note that the wise rhymes on the font were put there by the sole order of Robert Joyce then churchwarden."

Nearby Tolleshunt D'Arcy can boast of John Henry Salter was born at Arundel in 1841 of well-to-do parents. By the time he was twenty it was clear that he had before him a great career in medicine. But he had an accident which meant he had to have a glass eye, and the only position he could hope for was as general practioner. Surgery's loss was our county's gain, for he chose Tolleshunt D'Arcy as the place to settle. He had kept a diary since he was eight, and not surprisingly the twenty-three-year-old newly-qualified doctor wrote, "1864, July 5. A practice down in Essex sounds exceedingly well," and recording later, "Reached Tolleshunt D'Arcy and sat down to dinner in the most cosy dining room in the world. Received with great cheering at the entrance to the village."

Within two days he had delivered his first baby and life took on the pattern it was to follow for more than sixty years. Despite the attractions of London to a man of his class he was always glad to get back to the peace and friendliness of his country practice. He also kept up his connections with sport and was a keen amateur boxer and followed all the championship bouts with great enthusiasm. Horse-riding and racing was a passion with him; he surrounded himself with dogs and cats from the outset; he took his hounds to coursing contests at which he was invariably successful. He was a man of such tremendous energy that he could indulge in all these interests while at the same time carrying out to the letter his responsibilities to his patients.

In October, 1872, when he was driving his trap through Kelvedon, he came up with, " . . . crowds of people carrying off wounded men and women from the railway accident which had taken place one hour before . . . " He spent seven hours at the scene. In November 1874 he proved his ability as a doctor by dashing to Goldhanger where a boat had capsized and, after four hours artificial respiration, restoring a man to life. By now he was well known in widely differing spheres. The *Lancet* was mentioning him as an authority on diphtheria at the same time as the King of Sweden was writing to order some of his dogs. When he was forty-nine he notes that he was up at six to do some gardening: an entry almost identical is made when he was in his eighties. Yet another entry rounds out his character: "1895. Sep. 12. Coming back from a confinement at midnight came across a chap lying in the road, dead beat—a tramp just out of prison. I scandalised my man by making him take the poor chap up and bring him home, walking myself, and then giving him a 'blow-out' of grub and a shilling! Wrong or right it gave me pleasure to do it, and did the poor old chap no harm." In January 1898, when he was fifty-seven he made the first of many overland trips to Russia, invited by the Muscovites to judge their great dog shows. He went shooting there, and a bear he shot was stuffed and sent home for him. It can still be seen, in the Chelmsford and Essex Museum. He contributed the "Wild Fowling" section to the *Victoria County History of Essex*. The saddest part of his diary is in 1904 when Dr Salter recorded the illness and death of his much loved wife. On his eightieth birthday the whole village assembled to pay tribute to him and express their gratitude in the shape of a silver lamp. He lived on to his ninetieth year and died peacefully the following April, to be interred in the village churchyard beside the remains of his wife.

Further north lie the Layer villages and Birch. At Layer Marney the Marney family established themselves in the reign of Henry II. They achieved eminence in public life and were responsible for rebuilding the church around 1500. The family tombs, dating from 1414, are very impressive with full-length terracotta effigies. Their house was to be even more impressive; the gatehouse was built with four towers higher than anybody else's at that date, but it was a status symbol with nothing behind it, for the house itself was never even begun, because the family line became abruptly extinct in 1525. The old gatehouse still stands, four-towered, eight storeys high, dwarfing the hall and the church which stands beside it among the trees.

The church of Layer Breton was built as recently as 1923 as the old church was damaged beyond repair by the great Essex earthquake of 1884. Layer de la Haye church overlooks the big Abberton reservoir which certainly was not there when the church was built in the fourteenth century. It holds five and a half million gallons of water, takes it name from the village of Abberton at its north-east tip and reaches four miles south-west, with a circumference of twelve miles.

If I seem over-enthusiastic about Heybridge it is because I love boats and all the sights and smells that go with them, and Heybridge offers that very mixture even as you cross the bridge which connects it to its town neighbour, Maldon. This is the "hey" or "high" bridge from which the village was named; until it was built, around the time of the Conqueror, the place was called Tidwoldington after its Saxon owner.

The road bends alarmingly through the old village centre past the church on the left, which is hemmed in on three sides by the development over the years of the original Bentall iron foundry and works, but even this industrial proximity cannot rob it of its glory as an almost complete bequest from the Normans. Straight ahead, down Hall Road, one can pass a nucleus of cottages and pub which perpetuates the atmosphere of old Heybridge and arrive at the Hall, which is a timber-framed, plastered house still looking attractive after five hundred years. The road peters out on the saltings, where ultra-modern summer chalets give this old-gravel works site the air of a pioneer frontier village. The main road swings round and climbs up to the Wave bridge, to cross the tail end of the Chelmer and Blackwater canal. By the bridge stands the local landmark, the big warehouse built in 1863 for the rapidly expanding Bentall business. For a warehouse it is considered a well-designed, even beautiful building which is noted in the reference books as worthy of preservation.

The village spreads on out to the popular caravan and chalet site at Mill Beach, with one or two old farmhouses looking a bit awkward in among the later Council houses. A right turn almost reluctantly indicated by a sign on a lamp-post goes down past little bungalows and chalets very reminiscent of Canvey Island, to bring you to the Basin, a small place, hardly part of the village. Park the car by the *Jolly Sailor*, which is below the level of the dyke, wander over to the ramp, climb up to the sea wall to appreciate the place fully and see the wonderful view. In the foreground there is a fascinating variety of small boats anchored off the hard and the last lock of the canal, with massive gates to outwit the ebbing tide. In the dock thus created you can see an interesting assembly of craft old and new, large and small; Dutch boats, French boats, English boats and barges, whose lines declare their glory in a bygone age, the survivors of what was once the commonest craft on Essex waterways.

If you are as lucky as we were there will be a timber ship from Denmark on the opposite bank, and in the pub the added flavour of foreign sailors speaking a strange language. Beside the dock old houses stand in company with the *Ship*, beautifully kept by owners who appreciate their good fortune in living here. On the way home ponder on the fact that this little bit of coastline was industrialised long before factories were thought of. Out on the flats ancient man dug salt pans, collected the sun-dried salt and travelled inland with it, to exchange it for flints and other necessities from the men of the West.

Marney Towers, Layer Marney.   *Walter A. Blythin*

Ten miles from Chelmsford, sixteen from Colchester and only forty miles from London, Maldon has its share of commuters. The estates growing out around the town are proof of the popularity of this place in today's world, and that may be because Maldon still keeps in its heart that individual character which gives visitors the chance to savour the atmosphere of an English borough which has been a thousand years a-growing.

Maldon does not rest on the laurels of a Roman glory like Colchester or Chelmsford, though there have been finds enough to show that those great empire-builders tramped this way. Maldon's fame is from a few hundred years later, when the Saxon tribes looking for new lands at the end of the fifth century came up the estuary of the Blackwater and found the perfect place for settlement.

The importance of that place is enshrined in its name—"Maeldun", or Hill of Assembly, the place where the people of the tribe gathered to settle their differences, plan the future of their settlement and to mete out justice. That hill, and traces of a defensive rampart thrown up around its summit, can be seen to the northwest of the town via London Road where, on the right, Lodge Road looks down into the valley of the Chelmer. The rampart was probably raised to the order of King Edward the Elder, in an effort to prevent increasing invasions by the Danes who tried to pass up the river on their plundering expeditions.

Sailing barge *Kitty*, built in 1895 for Horlocks of Mistley. It carried barley, malt and cattle food until 1955 and is now used for holiday charter work.

Russell Edwards

80

It is the record of just such an expedition which has taken the name of Maldon round the world and down the ages. Back in 991 a gang of Danes beached its boats on Northey Island in the estuary of the Blackwater, but they were surprised by a great force of Saxons gathered on the mainland. The Saxons, however, lost their great advantage when they allowed the Danes to cross over the causeway at low tide and form up again to do battle. The Viking raider inflicted a disastrous defeat on the Saxons, who fought so bravely that their deeds were celebrated in a poem which was recited by minstrels in the halls of the warriors all down the years until it was finally written down—to be preserved in our literature as The Battle of Maldon—one of the first known poems in our language, though it has to be translated for modern readers.

Despite that temporary setback the settlement persisted and grew in importance. Proof of this can be found in the Domesday Book where Maldon gets more than one entry. In them it is clear that much of the land had been held by the King, so it is not surprising that the granting of a charter to Maldon by Henry II in 1171 made it the first Essex town to be thus honoured. One condition was that Maldon should provide a ship towards the defence of the country, and that ship has taken its place in the town's coat of arms.

At Maldon Hall, on the left as the approach road to the town bends right, are the remains of two moats indicating the medieval origin of the site, when ditches were dug to show the extent of ownership, to drain the site, and to act as a deterrent to would-be invaders. The old Maldon West railway station next appears on the left, looking rather sad since the line was abandoned, though the track it followed has become a new-style nature reserve.

The houses crowd round the space on the right where the twelfth century Hospital of St Giles for lepers now stands as a roofless ruin. Roman bricks can be detected in its walls which makes it an interesting spot archaeologically, but it is hard for the imagination to re-create the scene when these poor infected inmates gathered round the monks who tended them. The town's nucleus is past the five-road junction, where the High Street offers facades of buildings all down the centuries. The general view can be enjoyed before turning aside to take in the picture of All Saints church on the corner at the top of the street. Look closely and you will see that while all the lovely large windows date from the fourteenth century, each one is different from the next. The buttresses between these windows have been embellished with statues of famous men of Maldon. They include Mellitus and Cedd, the missionary bishops who brought Christianity to the Saxons, Brithnoth, the valiant Saxon leader at the Battle of Maldon, and Robert Mantell, twelfth century founder of Beeleigh Abbey. That abbey, northwest of the town, down by the Chelmer and now in the possession of the famous Foyle family of booksellers, can be visited on Wednesday afternoons. The images of Sir Robert D'Arcy who gave the Moot Hall to the town in 1440, and of Dr Plume who left the town his library in 1704, continue the story.

All Saints has another unusual feature, a three-sided tower built in the thirteenth century which is now the oldest part of the building. In the cool interior there are so many points to note that I would refer the visitor to the excellent guide available. Look for the vicarage behind the church and you will sense a real shock of delight at its timber and plaster facade— a truly lived-in fifteenth century gem. Across the street the *Blue Boar* conceals behind a late eighteenth century front another old

Moot Hall, High Street,
Maldon.

Owen Keen

timber-framed building. Its early construction shows in the beams of the old stabling through the archway. The sign denotes the connection of this inn with the powerful De Vere family, Earls of Oxford, for it is their family badge. Next, on the right of the High Street, stands the *Kings Head*, its buildings a story book in themselves through all the years from Tudor times when it began as the hall-house now hidden behind a brick frontage of the eighteenth century modernisation. The next building of interest is the Moot Hall which started off with D'Arcy's plain brick tower put up in 1440. The porch which now spans the pavement on four columns was built about 1830. Here in the centre of local government was kept the wonderful series of town documents from 1383, now removed for greater safety to the Essex Record Office. The clock which juts out so boldly on its bracket was the gift of another famous Essex man, George Courtauld, in 1881.

At the corner of High Street and Market Hill stands the tower of the old St Peter's Church. The rest of the building, by then quite dilapidated, was removed in 1665. Dr Thomas Plume, a Maldon man who became Archdeacon of Rochester, had a two-storeyed structure built back on to the tower around 1700. On the ground floor his old grammar school was able to take on a new lease of life and above it he gathered his own library, largely theological, amounting to some 6,000 volumes which he bequeathed to the use of the townspeople forever. The wonderful library can still be visited through the little door in the base of the tower and up the worn, spiralling stone steps. Through that door one steps back three hundred years; bookshelves and furniture are contemporary, stained floors, rush mats, the very bindings of the books in leather add to the atmosphere.

It takes no time at all to walk down the hill to another cluster of old houses round St Mary's church in the third of Maldon's ancient parishes. The church placed high on the bank of the Blackwater looks out over the estuary. Entries in the registers show that Scottish lads and lasses who had moved down to Maldon with the herring fleet met and married Maldon folk, and for such seafarers the tower has been a landmark through six hundred years. Below it the *Jolly Sailor* offers refreshment and interesting views, followed by a stroll along the old quay. The barges, with their tall masts, brown sails and complicated rigging make a most attractive group. One of them is preserved as a training ship for Sea Rangers, others have become the permanent homes of people who just love the life. It is only a step further along to the modern amenities of boating pool, open air swimming pool and public gardens through which it is possible to walk back to the town. Going the other way from St Mary's there is a pleasant walk past the old boat sheds which climbs up Downs Road to the footpath high above the River Chelmer. Halfway along this path stand the black, tarred sheds in which the Maldon salt industry is still carried on. The river here is extra salty when the high tides scour the saltings. From this water salt has been obtained by evaporation in huge vats for a hundred years or more; but it is an industry with a much longer history. The "red hills" found along this creek-gashed coast prove that salt-making was carried on even in prehistoric times. Today the Osborne family, using simple techniques with strict controls on hygiene and quality, produce boxes of salt in beautiful, big crystals for the best tables in the country and abroad.

Maldon Quay   *Owen Keen*

The walk ends by the bridge, where one can watch the unloading of timber boats from Aarhus and other romantically sounding places, which keep up Maldon's reputation as an ancient port. From here the Market Hill can be climbed to complete a circular but by no means comprehensive tour. There is more to Maldon. The burial register of the church of All Saints tells the story of a memorable Maldon man:

"1750. Edward Bright, a tallow chandler and grocer of this town, was buried the 12 November, 1750, in the parish church of All Saints near the belfry door. He weighed upwards of 42 stone (horseman's weight). His coffin was 3ft. 6ins. over the shoulders, 6ft. 7ins. long and 3ft. deep. A way was cut through the wall and the staircase to let it down into the shop; it was drawn upon a carriage to the church, slid upon rollers to the vault made of brickwork, and interred by the help of a triangle and pulley. He was 29 years of age the 1st March last, has left a widow now big with her sixth child. He was a very honest tradesman, a facetious companion, comely in his person, affable in his temper, a tender father, and valuable friend."

In life Edward Bright was more than a local curiosity; such was his bulk that pictures of him were sold throughout the country and abroad, often with interesting details attached, like the print which bears the legend, "He was an eminent Shopkeeper of that Town & supposed to be the largest Man living or perhaps that ever lived in this island; he weigh'd Six Hundred one Quarter and twenty one Pounds, computed to be about five Foot nine Inches high, his Body was of an astonishing bulk, & his Legs were as big as a midling Man's Body and though of so great a weight and bulk, surprisingly active.

N.B. A Wager was proposed between two Gentlemen of that Place & determined December the first 1750, which was that five Men at the age of 21 then resident there could not be button'd within his waistcoat without breaking a stitch or straining a button which when it came to tryal not only ye 5 propos'd but 7 Men were with the greatest ease included."

This is one of those cases where we can truly say, "Like father, like son", for that same burial register reports forty years later, "1790 Edward Bright, tallow chandler and merchant of this town, was buried . . . in the family vault . . . 28 March 1790 in the 45th year of his age. He was supposed to be about half the weight of his late father . . . He was brought to church on the bier by ten men and interred by the help of a triangle and pulleys. He left a widow and nine children. He was a man very much respected by a numerous acquaintance and a valuable friend to Society." With all those children it is possible yet that from some still-living branch of the family a Bright may be produced to break even this record.

Not so long ago the river at Langford could only be crossed by getting your legs wet, or standing on the back of your horse. The place derives its name from the "Long ford" which the Saxons had to negotiate. The waterworks here were in use by 1927 and water drawn from this area is delivered to the Hanningfield Reservoir by the action of a big pumping station and a nine-mile underground pipe. As the waterworks are vital in our daily life, so was the church of St Giles in earlier days when every settlement was practically self-sufficient. Then this building, the pride of the place, was the town hall, theatre, law court and committee room as well as serving its prime purpose as a place consecrated for Christian worship. The church as it stands now is the result of a well-meaning restoration of 1882 which completed urgently needed repairs, but rather spoilt the original character. However it did not alter the church's one great claim to the visitor's attention, the apse at the west end, a feature which is now unique in this country. An apse has been well described as, "the semicircular or polygonal end of the choir or chancel in certain churches." As it is usually the choir end of the church you will have gathered that it is under the east window, but that is where St Giles' differs, although it did at one time have an apse at both ends; the outline of the eastern apse was discovered when the chancel was extended.

Along with the buildings—church, mill, Valley House which show how history has marched through Langford—there is one man whose name has not been forgotten. He is that "Thomas of Langford" who was born here and grew up to be a Dominican friar in the Priory at Chelmsford. He became one of the best-known theologians of the early fourteenth century, and is also famous for his history which he called a *Universal Chronicle*.

Woodham Walter is "a picturesque village and parish bounded on the north by the River Chelmer and watered by a rivulet."* The Saxons chopped a settlement out of the forest, and Woodham means exactly that. The Norman conqueror distributed lordships of the Essex manors to the most deserving of his knights and Walter, who gave his name to the dynasty of the Fitzwalters, received Woodham. Its church stands all alone now. It was built in 1563, a very late date for the building of parish churches and imitates in brick an architecture classified as Perpendicular which you would expect to see carried out, in stone, at least a century earlier. The font within is a fifteenth century relic of the earlier church on the same site. Half a mile to the south there were to be seen the remains of a great, fortified house in a nine-hundred acre park. It was the home of the Fitzwalters and Queen Mary, as a princess, stayed here in 1550 when she was in fear of attempts on her life and a boat was kept in constant state of readiness at Maldon to take her to the continent at short notice. But you will not find a stick or stone of it today, for the Fitzwalters acquired the even more splendid New Hall, Boreham, and the old hall, passing into other hands, was demolished. Past the church the road dips down to give a particularly good view of the old inn, the *Bell*, standing in the valley of that rivulet which helps to swell the Chelmer.

The landmark for miles around is the slim spire of St John the Baptist, the church of the neighbouring parish of Danbury which crowns the hill, at a height of more than 350 feet. The Ordnance Survey map gives a wonderful picture of the place; from the boundary just across the Sandon Bridge on the A414 up the ever-increasing incline of Danbury Hill, past Danbury Palace and the *Bell* and even steeper again to the war memorial and the *Griffin*. Opposite is the lane which climbs yet higher to the church and the ancient earthworks which look out over the common to the south. To the north houses quickly give way to the scenery of Lingwood Common, while to the east, past Eves Corner, there is Runsell Green, an ancient hamlet with its *Anchor Inn* and the choice of two pleasant routes to Maldon.

Sir Walter Mildmay, founder of Emmanuel College, Cambridge and Lord of the Manor in Elizabethan times, built Danbury Place in a large deer park. The Hearth Tax return of 1662 shows that it had no less than 22 fireplaces. His descendant, Sir Humphrey Mildmay, born in 1593 was an important man in Essex, but he backed the wrong side in the Civil War, and so stayed at home in his big house, gambling and drinking with the Rector, Clement Vincent, who had been thrown out of the living by

*Kelly's *Directory of Essex*, 1937.

85

View from the Danbury War Memorial, 1973.

the Puritans, until his estates were themselves seized and he had to pay more than a thousand pounds to redeem them. His diary has entries which transcend time and engage our sympathies today. In 1641 he writes, "After dinner my woeman and I did fall out ill-favouredly and so we both continued sulky till worthily I did acknowledge all error to be mine, when all became well again, and we to supper and bedd."

Danbury Place sheltered a good many families down the years, descending to the status of a mere farmhouse. In 1831 John Round bought it, pulled it down and built the present house now known as Danbury Palace. It was designed by his wife, Susan, who, because she had a great fear of fire, insisted that three staircases, one entirely of stone, should be included. Tragically she died by fire in a London hotel. She went back upstairs to retrieve a valuable bracelet, and was trapped. Her body was brought home to lie in the churchyard in a grave which is still marked. John Round could not bear to live in the house and since the Church was looking for a palace for the Bishop of this diocese he was able to sell it to them for £24,000.

The Bishop of Rochester, to which diocese Essex was then attached, added, in 1860, a chapel to his large house which already included, "all the motifs of Tudor architecture . . . square and polygonal towers, stepped gables with pinnacles at the apex, mullioned and transomed . . . windows . . . arranged . . . without any noticeable principle other than picturesqueness."* A revision of diocesan boundaries made the place redundant so it was sold in 1892. Between then and 1903 one owner cut down 429 oaks and the character of the old place was changed beyond recognition. It is now a centre of management training and new residential and studio blocks have been built in expensive materials to harmonise with the playful Victorian gothic. There is a back door from the palace grounds leading straight to the lakes which went, as a moat, with the old house. Public access to them is from the Sandon road where there is a car park.

In the church you will see memorials to the St Clere family, dating from about 1300 and including life-size effigies carved in oak, which have a fame far beyond the county. When one of the coffins below them was opened in 1779 the corpse was discovered to be "lying in a liquor or pickle, somewhat resembling mushroom catsup,

* N. Pevsner, *The Buildings of England—Essex*.

but of a paler complexion and somewhat thicker consistency", which one of the company had the nerve to taste! Coller's* description concludes, "Whether it bore the characteristic mark of a dead crusader was not ascertained, as some ignorant and meddling bystander thrust down his stick, and broke off one of the feet at the ancle. The coffins were again religiously closed, and the body re-consigned to its long resting place."

Round the corner of the main road and on past the little thatched branch library, once the village school, burnt down in October, 1984, is the pond at Eves Corner where a lane goes down the hill to Little Baddow. In the church at the bottom of the hill there is a large wall-painting of St Christopher which was done five hundred years ago and restored from beneath layers of plaster and lime in 1920.

Danbury Branch Library, 1974.

When, in the seventeenth century, the Reverend Thomas Hooker was driven out of the church at Chelmsford and excommunicated because of his Protestant views he and his friend in that church, John Eliot, moved out to Cuckoos Farm in this parish and set up a school. On Sundays they preached to folk who dared to come from miles around to share their kind of Christianity. Eventually both men went to America seeking freedom in religious belief. Hooker went in 1633 and became one of the founding fathers of the American constitution. Eliot went to minister to the Indians, translated the Bible into their tongues and earned himself the sobriquet of "Apostle to the Indians."

On the other side of the hill stands Sandon. Its church has a strong tower in Tudor brick with an interesting stair turret which rises through the trees in picturesque fashion. The tradition is that it was built by Cardinal Wolsey, and this could be so because he was granted the manor of Sandon by Henry VIII. In the church one of the most striking features is a painting of the patron saint, St Andrew, done in bold,

*The People's History of Essex, D. W. Coller—1861

modern style. It connects with Rose Cottage on the road to Danbury, for here, until his death in September 1977 lived Mr Lynton Lamb, painter and designer. His widow, Mrs Barbara Lamb, told me how they came to their cottage as a young married couple at the end of 1940. Back home after the war Lynton started up village cricket again, became chairman of the parish council, was elected a churchwarden and, in the 'sixties, founded the Sandon Society. All these activities were in addition to a busy life as painter, designer, book illustrator and lecturer. He not only wrote books on painting like *Drawing for Illustration* and *Materials and Methods of Painting* but also the charming *Cats Tails* which he illustrated as well, and several detective stories such as *Death of a Dissenter, Picture Frame* and *Man in a Mist*. Two of his paintings hang in the Chelmsford and Essex Museum.

Over the humped-back bridge the road ahead rises to the hamlet of Woodhill where Woodhill House stands in charming seclusion—a seventeenth century brick facade with Dutch-like gables and additions through the years. It is the family home of the Raschs. The pool at the back of the house was dug out by French prisoners of the Napoleonic wars.

The B1022 from Maldon to Colchester gives access to three villages south of the A12. Wickham Bishops and Great Totham merge today as estates have been developed to provide countryside homes for town commuters down these two main roads. Wickham was already a manor belonging to the Bishop of London when the Domesday Book came to be written, hence its name. On the River Blackwater, among the trees, stands Wickham Mill, one in a series of buildings on this site which goes all the way back to the Domesday record. The house called Wickham Place, the mill beside it and the river moving in a wide pool make a delightful view. One must continue on the B1018 high above the mill to find the origins of Wickham Bishops' history in the old Norman Church, now in ruins, which is found down the rough road which crosses the disused railway track. Wickham Hall, nearby, keeps its water-filled moat on three sides. The road opposite, by Wickham Hall cottages, goes up to a copse with the unlikely name of Likely Wood and takes one to the top of the hill where a right hand turn leads past the present church which in its style looks much older than its one hundred and thirty-odd years.

The village itself has spread all about the many road junctions encountered up the road east of the church. One villager pointed out the reason for this maze, "In the old days there were two pubs on the road down to Great Totham and everybody took the shortest cut across the green to get to them. Each man made a regular footpath from his door to the inn and when the county council took them over they turned them all into roads." A likely story! But, after all, was it not Chesterton who said, " . . . the rolling English drunkard made the rolling English road"?

Great Totham gathers in several nuclei around the slopes of Beacon Hill. One of its claims to fame is that Charles Clark was one of its sons. He lived here as a tenant farmer up to about 1860, then retired to Heybridge, dying twenty years later aged seventy-four. He was an enthusiastic amateur printer, producing a long series of pamphlets and other material including his own edition of Thomas Tusser's *A Hundreth Good Poyntes of Good Husbandrie*. With his neighbour George Johnson he compiled and printed a history of the village. It was his quirks of character which made him famous in his own time. For instance, he would write verses, attach them to balloons and send them off on their own individual journeys of propaganda. He was a bachelor with a fervent belief in the need for birth control in our country. He even produced in 1843 a revised version of the national anthem which began, "God stop Quick Vic, our Queen"! His works on the locality are valuable today as vignettes of local manners and customs, including *John Noakes and Mary Styles; or, An Essex Calf's Visit to the Tiptree Races.*

Tiptree's races have long since been abandoned and its reputation now rests on jam, though it can be said on the side of history that it boasts a windmill, and, away to the southwest, the evidence of a Tudor mansion where Tiptree Priory now stands. It is in the fields all about that the local industry is most evident. Strawberries, raspberries, soft fruit of all kinds are to be seen growing and all destined for Wilkin's Tiptree preserves. Arthur C. Wilkin, farming at Trewlands, built the factory in 1885 which still operates. The adjoining farm of Tiptree Hall also came into the business. This is the farm on which J. J. Mechi once lived.

Of him John Booker, in *Essex and the Industrial Revolution* has this to say "His descent into Essex in 1841, like some *deus ex machina* for the salvation of agriculturalists, was one of the amazing incidents of Victorian Essex. He was the third son of a naturalized Italian and by 1840 he had realised enough capital from the sale of his 'magic razor strop' and patent lamp for the illumination of shop window fronts, to buy Tiptree Hall Farm for £3,400. By deep drainage, fertilization and the careful use of a horizontal steam engine, he was able to turn a traditionally barren and bleak heath into a sound and profitable farm. He was elected an alderman of the City of London in 1858 and would probably have become Lord Mayor if his disastrous business associations . . . had not ruined both his standing and his capital. His affairs were placed in liquidation in 1880 and he died a year later.

Mechi's importance lies in his scientific approach to farming and the enthusiasm with which he pursued it. The traditonally leisured and cautious improvements of the earlier landowners contrast with his frenetic efficiency at cost and benefit analysis . . . "
" People came from all over the world to learn from his revolutionary methods of agriculture."

Tiptree windmill.

Owen Keen

CHAPTER EIGHT

Wandering Westward from Aldham

ALTHOUGH Philip Morant's remains lie in the wilderness of the old churchyard at Aldham his tombstone has been brought into the chancel of the present church, where a window and a tablet also remind the visitor of the great contribution this sometime humble rector made to Essex history.

From Aldham the A604 twists and turns in the valley of the Colne to Earls Colne. This pleasant village was named after the De Veres, Earls of Oxford, who lived in the hall next to the church. One of its most interesting features is the humble old village pump. It was built into a very handsome edifice over a well dug in 1853 as a memorial to the escape of the majority of the population from a virulent outbreak of cholera which swept the county.

It was here that the infamous Thomas, Lord Audley of Walden, was born in 1488, but a man who made more contribution to this, his native place, was Reuben Hunt. Born in 1836, he spent his whole life in the village and died in 1927, a venerable nonagenarian whose kindnesses will long be remembered. He started the Atlas engineering works, following in the footsteps of his father Robert. The works employed so many people that the place grew to the proportions of a town. Hunt's philanthropy included the building and equipping of a chemical laboratory at Earls Colne Grammar School in 1893. As an ex-pupil he was pleased to add other extensions, including a complete carpenter's shop. In 1904 he paid more than the County Council itself in the building of a block to contain additional classrooms and laboratories. In 1913 he presented to the village its Hall, capable of seating over 300 people.

There are no Roman remains in Halstead but coins found here prove the antiquity of the settlement. Its position was recognised by the Saxons who called it a "healthy place", and in their language, "Halstead" it has been ever since. The church they built was ruinous before written record. The earliest part of St Andrew's, at the top of the hill, dates from the fourteenth century.

As there is no stone in Essex the builders turned to the material most readily available—flints, using the expensive imported stone to dress the corners and support the apertures. From the oldest part, the nave and its aisles, built about 1320, to the newest, the square tower with its attractive battlement and pinnacles, erected in 1848, there is a continuity of preservation of this building which was, right up to our own times, the very centre of town life. From those earliest days the Bourchier family ruled the roost as Lords of the Manor of Halstead. In the south aisle, once actually called the Bourchier Chapel, are the grand tombs, with effigies, of Sir Robert de Bourchier,

Lord Chancellor of England in 1340 and his son, Sir John, who died in 1400. Their present condition is indicative of the ages and the vicissitudes they have survived. Coller, writing in 1861, gives us an idea of those vicissitudes, "The mother church of Halstead is a large and noble edifice, with the stamp of venerable antiquity upon it; but for years it lay in a state of wretched dilapidation, with its roof shored up by wooden beams and its altar almost open to the winds . . . "

Though the tower is not very old, one of the bells is of the original sixteenth century peal and proves that the "low melodious din" sounding out across the fields was as good a timekeeper for the townsfolk as the BBC today. And ringing those bells was not always a wholly unenjoyable task. In the belfry there is an old bellringers' jug, dated 1658, capable of holding four and a half gallons of ale and inscribed, "If you be wice Fil me not twice At one sitting."

Holy Trinity church, built in 1844, at the other end of the town, reflects the increasing population as the town drew folk from the countryside in the industrial revolution. But Halstead, market town though it assuredly has been, and as such still preserves a pleasantly rural atmosphere, has been an industrial town for a very long time: in fact, ever since Edward III issued a decree forbidding the export of wool in order to encourage the new, young craft of weaving which Flemish immigrants had been invited to bring over and introduce into this district.

Sheep-farmers, wool-merchants and cloth dealers all prospered through the industry of Halstead weavers. Fresh waves of Flemish immigrants fleeing religious persecution continued the craft through the years and the "bays and says" of Essex, its famous serge cloth, was exported far abroad and more particularly to Portugal. The Civil War and the plague of 1665 so disorganised the woollen trade in Essex that the initiative passed to the northern mills and was never regained.

In 1782 George Courtauld, a descendant of one of those refugee Flemish weavers, first set up in Halstead as a silk throwster and gave rise to the later Samuel Courtauld and Company silk weavers who have become an international consortium. That first weaving mill, built across the Colne to use its water power, was still working right down to the 1980's. Now it is being developed as a supermarket, while preserving its outward appearance. The mill, found along the Causeway, is built all of wood, a typical Essex construction. It has rows of very large windows which were so designed in order that work might continue from early morning to dusk without interruption. Meantime the name of Courtauld has gone round the world— and is still quietly appreciated for acts of beneficence in Halstead, Braintree and Bocking. For instance, the Cottage Hospital built in 1864 at the expense of George Courtauld and the memorial in St Andrew's churchyard to the fallen of the First World War, though it appears to be of the fourteenth century, was paid for by Mrs S. A. Courtauld in 1920.

For its size Halstead has some unusually important industries besides that famous mill. My eyes were opened the day I toured Evans Electroselenium when Mr Arthur Evans, founder of the firm was still firmly in control. Not only was I amazed by the range of complicated photo-electric cell instruments made here, but I was also attracted by the very earnest endeavour to make the place as pleasant to work in as possible.

Who does not remember the tortoise stove? Any servicemen who crouched gratefully in front of one in a Nissen hut during wartime winters will never forget them. As a one-time reluctant serviceman I never realised that they came by the thousand from little old Halstead. But the Tortoise Foundry has gone on from those days and under the banner of Charles Portway & Son, Ltd. the tortoise has moved rapidly with the times, becoming a basic element in oil-fired central heating, and the firm has developed a whole range of applicances in oil and gas heating, while the old foundry has met modern competition with clever diversification of product.

This interest in metals is furthered by a number of engineering works which have gathered about the town, like Halstead Metal Works, KL Foundries and W.A. Hunwicks who claim they can make anything from a pin to an elephant. They proved the point by producing some full-sized mechanical elephants with petrol engine and gearbox which could carry up to eight adults and four children at a very realistic walking pace. So, out in the U.S.A. there is a weird pachyderm which advertises Halstead people's ingenuity.

The public gardens in Trinity Street were opened in 1901 to celebrate Queen Victoria's Diamond Jubilee: they contain a miniature lake, with a fountain, a bandstand, a large central lawn, and beautifully laid out flower beds.

Northwest of Halstead lie the Hedinghams, Castle and Sible. While Castle Hedingham climbs the relatively peaceful Nunnery Street up to the castle, sister Sible suffers the constant attack of traffic up and down its main street, the A604. The main road has brought modern industry and its necessarily functional buildings, and many villagers appreciate the pleasures of being able to live and work in the country. Around the church the flavour of the old village nucleus can be savoured in the view of old houses like Greys Hall, the *White Horse* inn, a house built in the fifteenth century and the later rectory with its classically pillared portico. It can only be surmised at this distance in time from its origin that "Sible" derives from a lady of that name, widow of Geoffrey de Laventon who held land in this area in the thirteenth century.

Hedingham Castle.

Owen Keen

Castle Hedingham's old houses and narrow streets in the protective shadow of the castle have brought tourists and so the shops of this one-time town have changed to suit this business—antique shops proliferate. They serve to point up the real history of a place where for six hundred years the De Veres, Earls of Oxford, ruled thousands of Essex acres in absolute, castellated authority.

The De Veres flourished in Essex from the time of the great invasion to the death of the twentieth Earl of Oxford in 1763. That first Norman lord was granted fourteen manors in Essex, together with much other property further afield. He founded a priory at Earls Colne and was buried there, although he had made his headquarters at Hedingham, where his son Aubrey, who died in 1141, built the castle with that massive keep. It was here that Queen Maud died. In gratitude for the family's support she made them Earls of Oxford and succeeding generations continued in high office under the crown.

The seventh Earl who died in 1360 "was one of the finest soldiers of his day," who saved England at the Battle of Poitiers by leading the English archers in their annihilation of the French. The nineteen-year-old ninth Earl accompanied the equally young King Richard II when he rode out to meet the rebels at Mile End during the Peasants' Revolt of 1381, and his uncle, who became the tenth Earl in 1392, carried the King's sword.

The thirteenth Earl of Oxford, John de Vere, was so active in the King's behalf that Henry VIII not only restored family fortunes and honours but added glorious titles, such as Lord High Admiral of England, Ireland and Aquitaine, Constable of the Tower of London and Castle Rising, and Knight of the Garter. But the Earl did not do everything right. There is the story told of the time the King stayed for a week

◀ Castle Hedingham. *Owen Keen* 93

at Hedingham Castle. Henry saw the large number of people lining the castle approach and said, "My Lord, I have heard much of your hospitality, but I see it is greater than the speech: these handsome gentlemen and yeomen which I see on both sides of me, are they your menial servants?"

"If it may please your Grace," replied the Earl, "they are most of them my retainers, that are come to do me service at such a time as this, and chiefly to see your Grace." The King then said, "By my faith, my lord, I thank you for your good cheer; but I may not have my laws broken in my sight. My attorney must speak with you." The point was that the Earl was seen to have more retainers in his private army than was allowed by the Statute of Retainers, and though he was so close to the King he had to pay a fine of 1500 marks.

The seventeenth Earl who lived from 1550 to 1604 has been claimed by one scholar, Thomas B. Looney, to have been author of Shakespeare's plays. On the death of the eighteenth Earl in 1625 the Essex link was broken and Hedingham Castle was no longer the family's home. The actual building to be seen today is the keep which guarded the entrance. Although in private hands it is open to the public during the summer months. The house beside it is Georgian. The moat which separates them is crossed by a fine-looking, well-preserved brick bridge built about 1500.

Down in the village the church echoes this structure with a brick tower of the same period, with all the exciting details of the time; diagonal buttresses, stepped battlements and a stair turret sticking up above them crowned with a cupola. The body of the church can nearly match the keep itself in its antiquity with the three twelfth century doors and early sixteenth century hammerbeam roof. This means the roof is supported by strong beams projecting from the walls and resting on wall posts and braced to form a bracket of great strength: Castle Hedingham's is one of only four of this kind in Essex. Under the seats of the stalls in the chancel you will find beautifully carved misericords with animals and humans depicted. A misericord is a bracket placed on the underside of a choir stall seat which, when turned up, provided the chorister with a support during long periods of standing.

Much building here has been done in brick because a large deposit of brick earth comes to the surface in this locality and has been made use of since Roman times. The clay at Southey Green and Gestingthorpe is particularly suitable for making tiles. Rayner's yard was established in 1893 and men walked from as far away as Sudbury and back every day to take advantage of the piecework rates which beat farmwork by twopence an hour. They got to Hedingham at six in the morning and worked a twelve hour day. The yard closed in 1952. Nobody kept a record of production, but even before the First World War it was estimated that over twenty million bricks had been made.

Westward lies the "open country of the people of Finc" as Reaney interprets our modern Finchingfield. That the Romans had a dwelling here is not surprising, for it is a sheltered, watered vale which would appeal to any prospective settler, and there are quite a few of the thousands of visitors who consider it the ideal place for retirement.

Roads from all directions descend to the village pond, where a humped-back bridge allows only one vehicle at a time. From the green beside the pond there is a view of cottages of all periods, and all beautifully kept, stepping away up the hill to the crowning glory of the church of St John the Baptist. To one side the old windmill raises white sails against an ever-changing Essex skyscape. There are so many points of interest, like the guildhall, now the parish hall which houses a small museum, and other old buildings such as the butcher's shop, Sculpins, Parsonage Farmhouse and of course, the church. Its tower is Norman, the steeple which once crowned it was blown down in 1658.

Half a mile down the lane off the B1057 at Duck End is Spains Hall, home of a former Lord Lieutenant for the county, Sir John Ruggles-Brise. This old and interesting house once had an owner about whom a curious tale is told. William Kempe lived from 1555 to 1628 and in 1621, in a rage of jealousy, he accused his wife of being unfaithful. Realising how wrong he was, he vowed he would not utter another word for seven years as a self-inflicted penance. Even after his wife died in 1623 he continued the terrible punishment. Each year that passed, so the story goes, was marked by the excavation of a fish pond in his gardens. There were once seven lakes to be seen in Spains Hall gardens. Today signs of them can still be detected, though only two remain, merged as one sheet of water. It is said by Sir William Addison that, at the end of that period of penance Kemp was in such a state of agitation that he became ill, and when he tried to call for help—he found he could not utter a sound. The shock killed him.

Spains Hall was bought by the Ruggles family in 1760, and passed to Thomas, son of Thomas Ruggles and Ann Brise whose maiden name was added to the family name through a royal licence obtained by their son in 1827. This man became noted for his concern for the condition of agricultural workers at the time of the depression at the end of the eighteenth century. His book, *The History of the Poor* published in 1797,

Finchingfield: "roads from all directions descend to the village pond".   *Owen Keen*

went through three editions. The line of Ruggles-Brise continued down to Sir Evelyn Ruggles-Brise, 1857-1935, who is remembered as a prison reformer as well as private secretary to four Home Secretaries. As chairman of the Prison Commission from 1895 to 1921 he pressed for reform of the treatment of young criminal offenders to such good effect that Borstal training was introduced in 1901. He is remembered in an inscription over the gateway to the first training establishment, at Borstal, near Rochester, which runs:"He determined to save the young and careless from a wasted life of crime. Through his vision and persistence a system of repression has been gradually replaced by one of leading and training. We shall remember him as one who believed in his fellow men." Thaxted is west of Finchingfield, through the attractive Bardfield villages. Great Bardfield boasts its own tiny cottage museum, where corn dollies in fascinating variety take pride of place.

Look at Thaxted from the junction of the B1051 and the A130; there is a lovely view down the hill and up again to the beautiful, soaring spire of St John the Baptist's church. It is a splendid church for such a small place. It reflects the prosperity that was here when cloth, its manufacture and sale was the county's greatest industry. That was five hundred years or so ago when men who amassed wealth were pleased to contribute to the adornment of their church.

Round the exterior are carvings and decorations under pinnacled battlements and the interior is light and airy with marvellous great windows which make you wonder how the roof can be supported. The fifteenth century font is enclosed in a case which rises in a cone of exquisitely carved tracery.

Of all its vicars down the ages, the man who is best remembered, or who achieved greatest notoriety, was Conrad Noel, who died in 1942. He was a confirmed Communist, though he was a grandson of the first Earl of Gainsborough. He was presented to Thaxted by the Countess of Warwick who became a champion of the socialist cause herself. He was a great friend of Gustav Holst the composer, who lived here from 1917 to 1925. Noel dared to hoist the red flag in the church; Cambridge undergraduates threatened to tear this down and for a while Thaxted was swarming with journalists. In later years this incident is said to have inspired the novel *The Flag* by Irwin Shaw. Noel's personality brought a vividness to church life over thirty-two years, and the Morris dancing which he and his wife re-introduced continues down to this day as a Thaxted speciality.

Behind the church two rows of old almshouses demonstrate the generosity of medieval merchants to the poor old people of the town. Unhygienic though they may look today, they must have appeared palaces to the widowed or handicapped agéd, and they have been sympathetically restored.

The windmill which rises above them has benefited from a recent campaign to effect its restoration. That is fortunate for it is a very striking feature on the skyline. Down the hill is the ancient guildhall looking new after one of the restorations and repairs which have kept it through five hundred years to delight modern visitors. The open space on the ground floor, framed by heavy timbers, was originally the market hall, while the room above was used for meetings of the town's guild of cloth makers.

The B1053 makes a scenic introduction to the architectural pleasures of Saffron Walden. On my first acquaintance with the town I drove twice round the place before I found the way to the market place. If you park on the common you can walk into Walden's history. At the eastern end of the common there is a maze cut out of the bare earth. You must walk all round its serpentine track, without jumping across the loops to solve the puzzle; that would be cheating. It is a humbling thought that more than two thousand years ago the members of some prehistoric tribe were treading the maze in all the earnestness of their religious belief that this complicated ritual would please the great god of fertility and bring abundance to their fields at harvest time. It says something for the town's concern for its history that the maze was being recut as far back as 1699 when it cost the corporation the handsome sum of fifteen shillings.

The soaring spire of St John the Baptist church and the ancient Guildhall: Thaxted.

Walter A. Blythin

Remains of Saffron Walden castle.   *Owen Keen*

Walk from the common to the top of the hill and you will come, on the left, across the remains of the castle ruined by Cromwell's Army. It is hardly recognisable now as the massive keep to the castle, built in about 1100 by the great Geoffrey de Mandeville, with ramparts stretching right out on the lines of Castle Street, Museum Street and Church Street. All the dressed, outside stones disappeared long ago, only the rubble infillings of those mighty walls survive to give us a quite inadequate picture of its original strength.

Archaeological evidence proves the earlier settlement in prehistoric earthworks now called the Battle Ditches off Abbey Lane, which the Saxons used as a cemetery, but the real importance of the place stems from the castle and the great stone church first built by the Normans, and the market literally stolen from the then thriving Newport in 1141.

The big market place was divided into lanes lined by the stalls, each row devoted to some particular ware, meat, bread, skins and so on. As the centuries passed the stalls became permanent structures, transformed into houses lining new streets. Butchers Row still survives to give an idea of how it all began and the present street arrangement in Saffron Walden is said to offer one of the best examples in England of the layout of a medieval market. As to the modern market place, I love the description in the town guide, "The pillared and heavily classic Corn Exchange has a remarkable clock tower of indescribable design, facing the indescribable fountain in the middle of the square." But in an age of box-like architecture I think both features have real character.

There is a more lively and fascinating introduction to Walden's past in the museum which almost adjoins the castle. The glory of this ancient town, the church of St Mary, is the largest church in Essex, 180 feet long and 80 feet wide, rising 193 feet to the tip of the spire. It is a beautiful building which reflects a very thorough rebuilding between 1470 and 1540, including the addition of a clerestory, which can be explained as an upper storey of the walls of the nave, pierced by windows. The very contract made with the freemasons in 1485 is still in existence and the building they produced is one of the finest examples of Perpendicular architecture in the country.

Though the spire seems so very much a part of the original design it is a modern addition put up in 1832 to the designs of Thomas Rickman, an eminent architect of the day. Each one of the memorials, in the floor and on the walls is a silent reproach to the indecent and rather pointless haste of modern life, for three-score-years-and-ten is but a minute in the span of time represented by monuments like that to Lord Audley, builder of the first great mansion at Audley End, who died in 1544. Local legend states that the unusual wooden lantern which preceded the spire was put up, as an experiment, by Henry Winstanley the great lighthouse pioneer. He merits further mention as an Essex born man. In fact his father was buried in the south chapel of this very church in 1680 though Henry lived at Littlebury.

Winstanley was born in 1644 and entered the service of the Howard family at Audley End, rising to be Clerk of Works there when James II was the owner. His interest in engraving brought forth a beautiful album of prints of the great house as it looked at that time. It has become not only a collector's gem, but also an invaluable contribution to the history of the place. His interest in "water-works" or fountains, which he showed in a London theatre, led him on to design the lighthouse which he hoped would withstand the storms of the Atlantic and guide the gallant seamen into Plymouth Sound. While building it he was captured by a French privateer, the crew of which destroyed all he had done: after his release, he persisted in the erection of the light. He was on the stark rock, in his lighthouse, when the great storm of November 1703 blew it, him and his assistants clear into the raging seas. None were saved.

Medieval houses in the High Street and Bridge Street show, in carved beams, lintels and window frames how some timbers were purposely left uncovered by the protective layer of plaster to show the skill of early woodcarvers. In recent times many a house has been stripped of that plaster coat, to show its wealth of timbers, thus exposing them to the agents of decay. In old photographs the *Cross Keys*, at the junction of King Street and High Street, can be seen without a beam showing, but in modern times its skeleton has been proudly revealed; a charming effect, maybe, but not a true restoration. This kind of work has done away with many examples of the Essex craft of pargetting, the raising of patterns or pictures in bold relief in the slowly drying expanse of plastered wall.

Look at the gables of the National Trust-owned cottages in Church Street. There is set out in bulging perspective a representation of Tom Hickafrith the Wisbech giant and Cambridgeshire folk-hero, carrying his usual weapon of a wagon wheel and axletree, confronting another giant with a huge club, whom he met and outsmarted on the road to Kings Lynn. At least that is what the local legend has been this last five hundred years. But how he ended up on a Saffron Walden wall defeats me.

99

Cottages in Church Street, Saffron Walden, showing pargetting.

Owen Keen

At the top of the hill behind the church and the museum runs Castle Street where the houses are charmingly varied in age and style, and all beautifully kept. From the street there are two passages which give on to Bridge End Gardens and the Anglo-American Memorial Playing Fields.

Surely it is unusual that a town should be named after a flower. Walden received its name originally from the Saxon settlement in the forest, but such was the importance of the cultivation of the saffron crocus here in medieval times that Saffron became its prefix, proudly carried ever since, and eventually incorporated in the town's coat of arms. But it was given recognition long before; in the carvings on the roof bosses in the church and on one of its arches.

Whoever discovered that the stigma of the purple flower of the saffron crocus produced a brilliant yellow dye has regrettably found no place in history. In the Walden area it is possible that a well-known figure in national history, Sir Thomas Smith, who was born in the town in 1514, was responsible for the development of the growth of the plant on a commercial scale. Philip Dickinson's useful handbook to the town tells how the saffron was obtained: "A man made a long, narrow trench with a special 'spit-shovel' in which women planted the 'heads'. When the flowers appeared, they were picked early in the morning into baskets and taken home where the stigmas were pulled out, the rest being discarded. These were dried in a special kiln and pressed into pound blocks, and the 'Saffron' was ready for sale."

It took about thirty thousand stigmas to make a pound of saffron which was also used as a medicine and a condiment. When better dyestuffs became available Saffron Walden gardens took a hard knock and by 1790 the industry was dead. It is a fact that in those early days roads in the town were completely blocked by heaps of discarded purple petals.

100

Industry does not make such a mess in the Saffron Walden of today, but it is thriving, tucked away on the industrial estate off the Thaxted road, bordered by the disued railway. There is still a main line station at Audley End and the glory of that great house can be reached by footpath from Abbey Lane.

Although it is called Audley End the house only has a connection with the Audley family because the Abbey at Walden was given to Sir Thomas Audley, Speaker of the Parliament from 1529 to 1535, for services rendered to Henry VIII at the dissolution of the monasteries. The house that he built, and the Abbey itself were demolished during the time that the estate was changing hands down to Thomas Howard, son of the fourth Duke of Norfolk. He was one of Queen Elizabeth's valiant sea dogs, knighted for his command of a ship that sailed against the Spanish Armada. He was further made Baron Howard of Walden in 1597 and continued in favour with James I, being made Lord Chamberlain, when he was largely responsible for the discovery of the explosives placed under Parliament by the gunpowder plotters. Amongst other honours and offices he was created Lord High Treasurer of England in 1614.

Thomas Howard built this great house but all records of its erection are lost, said to have been deliberately destroyed. It was supposed to have been thirteen years in the building, from 1603, and, it was rumoured, the Earl told the King it cost him £200,000 even in those days. King James is said to have replied that the house was too large for a king, though it might just do for a Lord Treasurer. The official guide tells us, "Since the 17th century the house has been the subject of much demolition and subsequent restoration and even partial rebuilding. As a result there is now little to be seen of the original structure . . . One of the noteworthy features of Audley End is that successive owners almost without exception have taken care to ensure that their own work should harmonise with the original 17th-century features. They succeeded so well that at first sight the new work may often be mistaken for the old."

Audley End. *Owen Keen*

One original feature is the Hall screen of 1605, one of the richest ornamented in the whole country. Any one can see it, for the house is now in the care of the expert inspectorate of ancient monuments in the Department of the Environment and open to the public. King Charles II bought Audley End for £50,000 in 1669 and established his court there from the following year. Successive Kings used New Palace, as it was called on a more occasional basis, but its purchase price had never been paid in full, so, in 1701, it reverted to the Howard family again.

The family line began to fail, the house became something of a burden. On the advice of the architect Vanbrugh, the great outer courtyard of buildings was demolished. He also made alterations to the existing fabric. The house passed into the hands of new owners in the person of Lady Portsmouth, and thus to her nephew who succeeded to the Howard de Walden barony and was created Baron Braybrooke in 1788. He expended the vast sum of £100,000 on the improvement of its, by now, parlous condition, and brought it largely to the appearance which greets our eyes today, though further improvements were made by the next owners, the Nevilles, early in the nineteenth century. There is a bonus for visitors. The Essex Record Office has rooms at its disposal to mount every year an exhibition from their priceless collection of records which touch on some particular period or aspect of Essex life and work. The grounds were planned by Capability Brown in 1736 and across the A11 the land rises to Ring Hill, an iron age camp on which Lord Braybrooke erected a "Temple to Peace", designed by Robert Adam, commemorating the end of the Seven Years' War in 1763.

Wendens Ambo village is off to the west down the B1039. Its name, Wendens Ambo, seemed so nostalgic to a BBC producer that a competition was arranged by "Woman's Hour" to find the best poem about the place whose name tells a little story. Back in the seventeenth century the inhabitants of the two small villages, Great and Little Wendens, were finding it harder and harder to keep their churches in repair. They petitioned the Bishop, Sheldon, and he took pity on their situation. One church and vicarage were pulled down, both were virtually ruinous, and the two settlements were joined as Wendens Ambo, their official Latin name, which merely means, both the Wendens. The church that was preserved, dedicated to St Mary the Virgin, makes the most marvellous setting along with the cottages at its gate. The Norman tower, the west doorway sporting Roman bricks and the remains of the murals discovered in 1934 and dated to about 1330 are three good reasons for saving it rather than its neighbour.

Newport was a very busy place on the great highway from London to Cambridge, with numerous coaching inns. The big church, also dedicated to the Virgin Mary, has many points of interest. One is the church chest, made seven hundred years ago. Its front is carved in a frieze of shields, circles and lozenges. But it is the painting of the underside of the lid which sets it apart. Here, largely in red and green are depicted the Crucifixion, the Virgin Mary and Saints John, Peter and Paul. Over the porch, high in the wall, there is an old sun-dial with a very modern-sounding inscription; "Many a man is well paid for abusing time" being a rough translation.

The school at Newport is of ancient reputation but few people know it was started by a woman. Back in 1581 Joyce Frankland, already widowed, lost her only son when he fell from his horse and received fatal injuries. The Dean of St Paul's sought to alleviate her distress by suggesting that she might "have twenty good sons" to comfort her and a new interest in life if she were to set up a school. When she died in 1588 she not only endowed Newport Grammar School but also founded scholarships at Oxford and Cambridge.

It is unusual to find that another well-known woman is connected with that school. She was the wife of one of its masters. Hannah Woolley was born in 1623 and married Mr Woolley, "Master of the Free School at Newport Pond in Essex" in 1647. He was a fortunate man for she was a good housekeeper and a clever writer on the subject. Her books on the art of housekeeping and pastimes for ladies were published from 1661 onwards and included the well-known *Gentlewoman's Companion*.

South of Newport lies the associated parish of Ugley and the parish registers of the two villages are kept together in a place of safety. The vicar was kind enough to show me them. From 1559 the record of baptisms, marriages and burials is kept, well or badly according to the clerk of the time. What caught my eye was a record of a very different kind, entered on the flyleaf, which gave me the merest glance into a vanished way of life:

"Musical instruments belonging to the Parish of Ugley. Base viol bot by subscription 1805 but the principal part paid by Sam. Leightonhouse Esq. of this Parish — of Oxford House cost £10-10-0 A violin given to the parish by Rev. Thos. Dalton Curate 4 Dec 1808 cost £6-6-0 The above two instruments in the care of Thos. Amey Gardner to S. Leightonhouse Esq of Oxford House."

The music made in a small village church at the time of Wellington's glory can well be imagined from this business-like account, entered in the one book which would be handed down to posterity.

The very name of the village brings its own difficulties. Whereas in every other place the Women's Institute is always preceded by the name of the place, this village has received special dispensation to call its branch the Women's Institute of Ugley!

Clavering is a scattered place with various hamlets, all in pleasant countryside, and a church built in the fourteenth century which makes a focal point in a setting of attractive houses, old and new.

A lane leads to Starling Green, the nicest name for the location of the nastiest crime — murder. In the Chelmsford and Essex Museum are the fragmentary remains of a pair of boots which were once a part of the "black museum" of the county constabulary, later transferred to the county town museum. These small boots belonged to Miss Camille Cecile Holland, a fifty-six-year-old spinster cruelly murdered at Moat Farm, Clavering, around 1899.

Samuel Herbert Dougal was a "cheerful anthropoid", an army man for twenty-three years who had delusions of grandeur and a wife and children to support. He resorted to forgery, was convicted and sent to prison, so he forfeited his army pension. On his release he lived on his wits, cheating gullible young girls out of their miserable savings by his charming manner.

He met Miss Holland in 1898 at the Earls Court Exhibition. She was an amateur poet and painter with a modest private income. He persuaded this more than middle-aged lady to buy Moat Farm in remote, rural Essex where, as lovers, they retired to live on the income from Miss Holland's £7,000 nest egg. She soon had enough of him and returned to lodgings in London. The landlady knew she had gone to see her former lover at the farm, but was told that she was no longer living there. This Mrs Wiskens learned from her former lodger's bankers and solicitors that Miss Holland had been drawing cash and effecting sales of shares quite regularly over the four years since she had disappeared. By 1903 the village was buzzing with gossip about the ill-matched couple and the missing lady.

The village constable began checking up all the facts known about Dougal, who had told Mrs Wiskens that Miss Holland was abroad, yet all those bank withdrawals and share sales had been signed by her. Dougal's previous record as a con-man and forger weighed against him, but he disarmed suspicion and went off to Bournemouth for the weekend with his latest paramour. When he did not return to the farm, but stayed in London and tried to cash some ten-pound notes, which were then very unusual, the police were able to arrest him for forgery.

While they had him under close supervision an all-out search was made of the farmhouse and gardens at Clavering. The digging of the garden to grave depth went on for weeks; even the ancient moat was drained, to reveal only a few fish floundering in the mud. The police were almost at their wits' end. If Dougal had disposed of his lover's body three or four years ago it was now going to be very difficult to prove it but they had a lucky break. The painstaking questioning, extended to just about everybody in the village, brought forward a farmworker who recalled that Miss Holland had come to the farm on 18th May 1899 because that was the day Dougal had told him to fill in the open drainage ditch which from time immemorial had traversed the farmyard. The ditch was excavated for most of its length before a piece of cloth came up, caught on the prong of the fork. The labourer dug again, the fork struck something hard, and he brought up a small lady's boot. The bones of the foot were still inside it. The rest of the body came to light, pitiful four-year-old remains which still revealed a bullet hole in the head. Dougal was tried and found guilty of her murder and hanged in Chelmsford prison on 14th July 1903.

"In the peaceful ▶
greenery of the
churchyard" at
Birchanger.

Sightseers at the
scene of the Moat
Farm murder,
Clavering, 1903.

In this part of the county there are so many places which could claim their place in this book, but space is at a premium, so they can only be glanced at in passing. Stansted Mountfitchet bestrides the busy A11. Its old tower windmill stands up above the houses, pricking the sky with its bold shape. The church is way out of town in what was once the grounds of Stansted Hall, where it was first built for that Saxon chief who decreed that his tribe would embrace the belief in this new One God. It has material and craftsmanship of all ages from Norman work down to the restoration of the nave in 1888. Monuments to the great people of the place begin with the early fourteenth century effigy of a knight in the north chapel, with his legs heraldically crossed.

There is one to Sir Thomas Myddleton, 1631, one-time Lord Mayor of London, who was buried here under one of the finest Jacobean altar-tombs in the country. Seven generations of his family were Lords of the Manor. Of course Stansted will be remembered from our day on for many a year as the place where the government wanted to develop a third London airport. Local opposition was so intense, so well organised and so general in the area that the idea was dropped, in favour of a site, to be called Maplin, reclaimed from the Maplin Sands off Foulness. But aeroplanes still circle the area on limited regular and charter journeys, and the shelving of the Maplin project through economic conditions today has caused the introduction of a scheme of limited local expansion.

The nearest village to the airport and its terminal buildings is Birchanger. In the peaceful greenery of the churchyard the way of life of an old Essex village can easily be recreated in the imagination. It was once in the ownership of William of Wickham, who included it in his endowment of New College, Oxford. St Mary's has a Norman nave and an Early English chancel. At its western end the bellcote is a nineteenth century substitute for the ancient round tower which apparently fell down and was cleared away without ever getting into the history books. Under the bellcote can be seen a curious round window, possibly of contemporary design, and under that again a Norman doorway which may well have been removed bodily from the north side, for it matches a south doorway only brought back to light in 1930.

Due south of Birchanger, across the A120, lies Great Hallingbury. It seems to dream peacefully enough of its past, despite the disruption of traffic and the carving up of the countryside in the engineering of the new M11. The village is scattered. Its church looks so old, yet all but the tower was rebuilt exactly a century ago. However, there is inside a very unusual clue to the age of habitation in this area. The chancel arch is in early Norman style, and made altogether of Roman bricks.

In the churchyard a great vault with sloping slab-like sides surmounted by a cross marks the last resting place of members of the Houblon family who descended from that Jacob who inherited great wealth, when he was but six years old, from London financier James Houblon, who died in 1700. Wright, the county historian in 1832 tells us, "Hallingbury Place, the seat of John Archer Houblon, Esq., is an elegant and stately mansion, on an eminence, within an extensive park, in a most pleasant part of the county . . . "and Lady Alice Archer Houblon in *The Houblon Family* gives us a very telling picture of the Lord of the Manor of 1891.

"But little remains to be told of John Archer Houblon. Rich and prosperous, he had a keen power of enjoyment which gave zest to all he did, whether of business or pleasure, and if he never spared himself in the former, he did not stint himself in the latter . . . a Tory of the Tories, and high and dry churchman of the old school, he was loyal always to the powers that be. He rebuilt the ancient white-washed church of Great Hallingbury, and spacious schools . . . he would tolerate no tenant on his estates but that he was a churchman. But in spite of his intolerance of all encroachments upon his ideal, 'The Squire'—and all Essex gave him this distinctive title as he grew hoary with age and dignity— was humble and tender as a child in his efforts to break his faults and school his life to the standard of duty he held above himself; for he had, as his friend the poet wrote of him:
'A nature loyally controll'd
And fashioned in the righteous mould
Of English gentleman!'
He would bare his grey head to wind and rain if the name of God crossed his lips or those of his companion; and there are those who remember the zeal, if not beauty, of his singing in church . . . and so, in a green old age, in 1891, this chivalrous squire of a past that is gone, slept with his fathers."

This estate was previously in the ownership of the Parker family from the fourteenth century up to 1697, when the line, which carried with it the barony of Morley, became extinct. The village is still sometimes called Hallingbury Morley from this connection. Henry, eleventh Lord Morley entertained Queen Elizabeth at Hallingbury Place in 1561 and again in 1576 but that was in the house which the Houblons demolished to rebuild in 1771.

"Little Hallingbury was a place of some manufacturing activity in the last century. A mill for twisting and winding of silk was then in full operation affording profitable employment for a large number of women and girls; but the clatter of its cogs is now hushed and the village has susbsided into rural quietude." That was written in 1862. In fact the mill began work in 1720 and was thus years ahead of the general establishment of the silk industry in Essex. It soon went out of business but it keeps its place in industrial archaeology because of the unusual water-drive engine which was installed.

West of Little Hallingbury and partly bordered by the road which crosses the Stort to the A11 are the ramparts which formed the bastions of Wallbury Camp. This great Iron Age fortified enclosure covers over thirty acres. The ditch alone varies between fifty and seventy feet in width, and its double rampart, nearly a mile in circumference, is a very unusual feature in such camps in Eastern England.

The B1005 leads to Hatfield Heath where the wide-spreading village green makes an ideal cricket pitch, at least from the spectators' point of view. Matching is a pleasant place to visit: but look for the insignificant signpost which points to Matching Hall and Church and you will be in for a delightful surprise. The narrow lane bends this way and that. Suddenly you are driving along the edge of a pond just about large enough to be called a lake. Water splashes through a little lock into the brook on the other side of the road, the wind rustles in the trees, the water birds swarm, about the the surface of the lake in amazing variety.

The little lake at Matching.

The church is just a little further up the lane, opposite the Hall, where a gate across the road indicates that it is, for the rest of its length, private. The church itself has witnessed the work of many hands, having been thoroughly restored about two hundred years ago and again in 1875 by the well-known architect Sir Arthur Blomfield. There are old features still to be enjoyed, like the pulpit, carved with vines and strapwork decoration, given to the church by Richard Glasscock in 1624, and the niche behind it where in times past people had to stand to do penance in sight of the congregation.

Opposite the church gate stands Matching Hall, whose age and interest cannot be concealed by the roses which riot up the walls and the rushes which turn its moat into winding ways for waterbirds. This moat was dug by Saxon settlers when the deep ditch could serve as a defence against Viking raiders, as drainage for the homestead site, and as a delineation of the property. That old hall, built and rebuilt, still boasts its Tudor dovecote and an old brick fishing hut.

Across the way is the oak tree planted to celebrate Victoria's diamond jubilee. But a sapling then, it now hides half the view of the church and its strong fifteenth century tower. Further on is the third interesting building in this very satisfying group. It stands against the church fence with a Victorian letterbox in its wall and a jutting upper storey which helps to prove its ancestry. Down the ages it has been called the wedding feast house because back in medieval times it was built to provide a place where poor people could have room to hold their wedding parties. The name of the worthy benefactor of generations of village couples is said to be Chimney, and that strange name is the only memory left of him. The lower storey is lived in today, but the upper storey is still used as a meeting room and Sunday School and the Vicar is pleased to show it to visitors. The Vicarage itself is an old house with later additions, hiding down the slope at the back of the church.

From this comparatively unknown backwater one can travel via Matching Green through five miles and a thousand years from old Matching to the New Town of Harlow.

CHAPTER NINE

Circling Round from Waltham Abbey to the Walthams

BESTRIDING the Lea and Stort navigation, the western-most settlement in Essex is Waltham Abbey. Here lived Thomas Fuller, the well-known church historian, whose work, *The History of Waltham Abbey,* was the first history of an Essex parish to be published, and that was in the middle of the seventeenth century. Fuller had a most illustrious antecedent here in Thomas Tallis who died in 1585. He wrote some of his best known musical compositions while he was organist in the Abbey, including the motet, "Gaude Gloriosa."

The Abbey is but a pale shadow of its former glory. All the monastic buildings have disappeared, and two-thirds of the Abbey itself. It has been rebuilt more than once, but tradition has it that King Harold's body was borne here to be buried in 1066. The site of his tomb cannot now be substantiated, but a black marble slab found in recent excavations is thought to be part of his sarcophagus. The associated settlement of Waltham Holy Cross commemorates the wondrous cross which Tofig the Dane was said to have carried here to the settlement on the edge of the forest, where he built a church to house it.

That forest, by a whim of history, still grows in the neighbourhood. People lived in dread of the advance of the new motorway but Epping Forest is thick and green just half a mile away. It did, however, suffer in the construction of this highway which made more inroads on the Forest than anyone has been allowed to for a long time. The great forest which once had covered Eastern England had been hacked back by the Saxons. As the population increased the forest became divided into patches. Epping and Hainault were separate forests which were increasingly threatened through their nearness to London. By 1848 it was proposed in Parliament that these two forests should be split among local landowners and cleared for cultivation or development. Hainault Forest suffered this fate, but the rights of the common people in Epping Forest could not so lightly be swept away, though legal argument was protracted. In the end the people won; the Epping Forest Act of 1871 preserved the forest to the public for their free use for ever and in this spirit it was officially opened by Queen Victoria in 1882. The event was of such importance that it was made the subject of a large mural in the County Hall erected in Chelmsford in 1931.

The Chigwell *King's Head* was chosen by Dickens as his model for the *Maypole* in Barnaby Rudge, published in 1841, and he wrote to a friend, "Chigwell my dear fellow, is the greatest place in the world . . ." Epping is so well summed up by Nikolaus Pevsner in his *Essex* that I quote: "The town of Epping itself lies outside the forest, to the NE. With the help of this *cordon sanitaire* it has never been swallowed up by London and keeps to this day its individuality as a small roadside town, with many inns and few streets . . . "

The best way to see the forest and its settlements is on foot; and most people would not believe that from near Loughton almost up to Bishops Stortford it is possible to walk continuously, mainly on public rights of way, for up to twenty miles. Essex County Council has recently produced a leaflet which gives full details of this walk, accompanied by a clear and large-scale map. Let me quote from this leaflet:

"A characteristic feature of the rural landscape of West Essex especially noticeable from the path is the isolated farmstead. Many of these are sixteenth or seventeenth century timber framed buildings often erected on the site of earlier settlements. Examples on the Forest Way are Parvills, Lea Hall, Corringales and Ryes in the parish of Hatfield Broad Oak. Lea Hall and Ryes are both mentioned in the Domesday Survey . . ."

A modern sculpture at Harlow.

The new town of Harlow is certainly a place worth seeing as Sir Frederick Gibberd's plans come to fruition in brick and concrete, and acres of greenery. It actually takes in Great Parndon, Little Parndon, Netteswell, Latton and the hamlets in between. There was of course, and still is, an old Harlow. Today its main street has been pedestrianised, an ugly word for a beautiful idea. Now it is possible to stroll down the street, admiring the older buildings, and crossing from shop to shop in safety.

The New Town has not only well designed, modern houses sited near to but not within the industrial areas, it also has a fully equipped sports centre, a golf course, water gardens and two parks for general recreation.

Hatfield Broad Oak preserves in its name a memory of the days when the forest enveloped the place, and the settlement was marked by a tree which was celebrated for its vastness in the Conqueror's time. In fact its alternative name, Hatfield Regis, is a reminder that William owned the land all about, and delighted in a day's hunting in the forest. Still marked on the map is the priory founded in 1135 by that same Aubrey de Vere who built the keep at Castle Hedingham. All that glory has gone, however, but for part of the chapel to the priory which remains as the west part of the parish church of St Mary the Virgin. In it can still be seen what is said to be the effigy of that noble founder, preserved in all his knightly splendour, though much defaced by time.

110

Hatfield Broad Oak in 1974.

A monument to Thomas Barrington, who died in 1472, shows how long that family has been associated with this village, for it was not until 1833 that the line, which, through marriage, quartered the royal arms of England, became extinct. It was in the library in this church that documents were recently found which showed that Robert the Bruce of Scottish fame was by inheritance Lord of the Manor of Hatfield Broad Oak. In more recent times the vestry was graced by no less a figure than the Reverend Francis W. Galpin. Whilst Vicar of this parish he assembled a supreme collection of old English musical instruments and wrote a book on the subject which was published in 1910. He went on to study old musical instruments of ancient civilisations and for his contribution to music scholarship he was made Honorary Freeman of the Worshipful Company of Musicians in 1905. Hatfield Forest is now owned by the National Trust, all 1,049 acres of it. It is possible to drive the car right to the very edge of the forest which makes it a very popular spot for picnics in the sunshine. It offers the opportunity of seeing those magnificent trees, the hornbeams, which are the pride also, of Epping Forest.

Dick Turpin, the notorious highwayman was an Essex man, born in Hempstead, east of Saffron Walden, where the entry of his baptism in the old, worn, register reads, in Latin: "1705. Sept,21. Richardus, filius Johannis et Maria Turpin." Such is the perversity of folklore that a sneaking admiration still exists for the masked gunman and his horse, Black Bess, though he was no more than a thug who ruled by the power of the gun and lived on the fruits of other people's industry. His father kept the *Bell Inn* at Hempstead and this may account for his falling into the low company of the district. It also showed him the wealth of folk who were constantly passing by on the main road and putting up for the night.

Indulgent parents pampered him even when he began work as a butcher's apprentice in Whitechapel. He collected a company of disreputable hangers-on, and lost his job. His marriage to Hester Palmer of East Ham was not the steadying influence his parents hoped for. He and his cronies became sheep stealers. Turpin's knowledge of butchery enabled him to kill and cut up for sale sheep and cattle. But he needed more money, so he took to housebreaking. On one occasion he and his gang rode one night from Chingford to Barking, stripping the two church vestries of everything valuable they could carry.

In 1730 the "Essex Gang" went one step further in assaulting owners of property. An old lady at Loughton would not tell them where her money was hidden so they put her on her own grate and scorched her into a disclosure which made them £400 richer. That was a fortune in those days, but it was eclipsed by the £700 haul from the home of a thrifty farmer at Rippleside, Barking. The gang was confident enough now to roam the Home Counties at will, and brought forth a royal proclamation for their apprehension. That caused them to lie low. Turpin escaped one attempt at arrest and decided to operate on his own. He was riding up the Cambridge Road, the A11, when he saw his first chance to be a highwayman. A single, wealthy-looking man was approaching. When Turpin told him to "stand and deliver" the traveller gave a great laugh. Turpin did not know it was Tom King, the renowned highwayman, that he was trying to hold up. "What Dog rob Dog?" said King. "Come, come brother Turpin, if you don't know me I know you and should be glad of your company". Later research has shown that once again folklore has changed the story, for in fact Turpin's accomplice at this time was a Matthew King. They spent three years of robbery together before King was shot resisting arrest. Dick Turpin carried on his infamous trade from a cave he fashioned for himself deep in the forest. A reward of £200 was offered for him dead or alive and he was forced to move north to Yorkshire to evade arrest. The only life he knew was by the gun and yet it was the shooting of a pheasant which brought him to book. He threatened a witness of the incident who never dreamed it was Turpin, for he was arrested in the name of Palmer. An indiscreet letter from jail brought recognition and he ended his life on the gibbet at York on 7th April 1739.

The Shell House: an eighteenth century pavilion by the lake at Hatfield Forest.

Where Hatfield Forest ends Takeley begins and it is a village quite split by the swift-running river of traffic which is the A120. The church, all on its own down a long drive at Brewers End, is large for such a small community. It was first built by the Normans, and some of the windows show the Roman bricks they made use of. Its much restored fifteenth century font cover is very tall, with lavish carving rising in a cone of pinnacles supported by arches and buttresses. This way we can come to the Dunmow villages.

Great Dunmow is large and busy enough to be called a small town, but architecturally speaking the town has little to offer, although it does have a car park off the main street, and a variety of shops, including a number of antique shops. To go to Church End one must pass the village pond, called Doctor's Pond. It was on this very sheet of water that models of the first self-righting lifeboat were tested back in 1785 by Lionel Lukin.

North of Dunmow are Great and Little Easton. The latter will be remembered as the home of Frances, Countess of Warwick. Valerie Flatley, writing about her in the *Evening Echo* in 1973 said, "Even in death the beauty of Countess Daisy lives on—frozen in a marble bust that stares sightlessly towards the altar of a parish church near Dunmow, Essex. Her hair, in an elaborate late-Victorian style, curls softly into the nape of the neck. The face is classically proportioned, the set of the chin proud, even haughty. An inscription reads: "Frances Evelyn Maynard, Countess of Warwick, Lady of the Manor of Estaines. Born: December 10, 1861. Died July 26, 1938." History could add: "Mistress of the future Edward VII, attempted blackmailer of George V, heroine of an Elinor Glyn novel and, perhaps strangest of all, committed socialist."

In death she lies in the Norman nave of Little Easton church, in life she had proudly sat there beside the future king who called her "My own adored little Daisy Wife". The bust is still a pilgrimage for the curious. Memorials to her ancestors, among them the armoured Sir Henry Maynard, granted the land for miles about by Elizabeth I, and his wife, Susan also attract attention.

Lady Warwick tells her own story in *Life's Ebb and Flo*; of how she was brought to stay in London when nineteen to be inspected as a future royal bride. But Edward, then Prince of Wales, encouraged her to receive the proposal of Viscount Brooke, heir to the fourth Earl of Warwick. "Daisy" came back into his life when she appealed to him for help in the retrieval of an indiscreet letter. Soon they were much together, often at Easton Lodge, and when they were apart they corresponded in lovers' language. Of his visits the Countess wrote, "How thankfully he threw aside for a few hours the heavy trappings of his state to revel in the love of nature." Little Easton at that time was a remote village, even though the railway had reached its neighbour.

For almost nine years Daisy was the Prince's "adored little Daisy wife" until 1898 that is, when one reason for the parting may have been the Countess's embracing of the socialist cause. She really did feel for the poor and uneducated. In 1897 she founded her own secondary school at Dunmow when only twelve out of a thousand Essex children had the chance of a secondary education. She presented the first grants to veteran miners and founded a women's agricultural college—and so the record of her generosity goes on. In 1923, when she was over sixty she even stood as a Labour Party candidate against Anthony Eden and lost.

But her earlier whirl of the good life had caught up with her. By 1914 she was not meeting her expenses. In her desperate situation there was one way out, to sell the Prince's letters to her. She let it be known that a publisher was willing to pay £100,000 for them, and offered through intermediaries, to sell them to the King. The royal family took legal action, however, and the letters were ordered to burnt in the sealed envelope which held them. Her intermediary, Arthur du Cros, was a gentleman such as is rarely found. Having seen that no smirch of scandal attached itself to the royal family, he also cleared Darling Daisy's debts himself, to the tune of £48,000.

The beautiful debutante was now, in the 'twenties, a stout dowager with little more than the grand home in which she lived. But her interest in the socialist cause never abated even up to her death in 1938. In that great "tottering mansion", which incidentally was ruined by fire and demolished in 1946, she still lived in splendour, owing bills to tradesmen for miles around. She took a lively interest in her neighbours and mentions famous people of the day with whom she had almost daily contact: Holst, Wells, Arnold Bennet, Clausen, and Conrad Noel to name but a few. Of her it would be fair to use the cliche that she certainly put Little Easton on the map.

Ralph Baynard is shown in the Domesday Book as being lord of Little Dunmow. It was his wife, or his sister, we shall never know precisely, who is said to have founded the Priory here in 1104, and charged it with the annual provision of the famous Dunmow Flitch. The present church, formed from the south aisle and five arches of the nave of the original priory church, preserves the only evidence left of that extensive priory. The earliest recorded award of the flitch of bacon was in 1444, when Richard Wright of Bradbourn in Norfolk successfully claimed it. The following ancient rhyme sums up the intention of the Flitch Ceremony:

> "You shall swear by custom of confession,
> That you ne'er made nuptial transgression;
> Nor since you were married man and wife,
> By household brawls, or contentious strife,
> Or otherwise, at bed or board,
> Offended each other in deed or word:
> Or, since the parish clerk said, Amen,
> Wished yourselves unmarried again;
> Or in a twelvemonth and a day,
> Repented, even in thought, any way;
> But continued true, in thought and desire,
> As when you joined hands in holy quire.
> If to these conditions, without all fear,
> Of your own accord you will freely swear,
> A whole flitch of bacon you shall receive,
> And bear it hence with love and good leave;
> For this is our custom at Dunmow well known;
> Tho' the pleasure be ours, the bacon's your own."

The Flitch Chair   First World War Memorial, Little Dunmow Church.

The ceremonial required the claimant to kneel on two pointed stones in the churchyard, and, after chanting and religious rites performed by the priors, make solemn oath of his marital harmony. "Then the Pilgrim, as he was called, was taken up in a chair on men's shoulders, and carried about the Priory church-yard, and through the town, with his bacon borne before him, attended by all the friars, and by the townsfolk, with shouts and acclamation . . ."

A trip around the village today is likely to be a good deal more staid, though another *Flitch of Bacon*, the hostelry of that name, still helps to bring a friendly spirit to the neighbourhood. There is the chair, too, which rather doubtfully is supposed to be the one used for chairing the winner of the Flitch. It is kept in the church which is unpretentious, long and narrow, a place for simple, sincere worship. One of its most splendid features is the tomb of Walter, Lord Fitzwalter, who died in 1431, and his wife Elizabeth. It is surmounted by their effigies, carved out in the formalised dress of their day with their hands folded in prayerful pose and their pet dogs curled up at their feet. From Little Dunmow the road runs on to Felsted passing on the way the Felsted sugar factory. Few people realise that Essex grows a great deal of sugar, in the form of sugar beet.

The lane from the factory comes down the hill to cross the Chelmer by Priory Bridge and rise to the giddy height, for Essex, of two hundred and fifty feet above sea level, where it meets the B1417 in the heart of Felsted. Straight ahead at the "T" junction on the B1417 stands the old school house, the nucleus of Felsted School, from which the complex of school buildings all around the village has spread in the last four hundred years. This old schoolroom housed the first few scholars when the school was originally opened in 1564, and the master lived in the house next door.

Through the archway under the schoolroom you come upon the church, tucked away behind the houses which line the street. It is a fine, large, all stone building and inside you will find, in the Rich chapel, all the family monuments including a real beauty to Lord Rich who died in 1568. It is all of various marbles and no less than fifteen feet high, with a finely executed effigy recumbent under an intricately carved canopy. Lord Rich, who became Lord High Chancellor to Edward VI, did as much as anybody to help in the transfer of church property to the crown after the dissolution of the monasteries, and was richly rewarded with twenty of the finest manors in Essex. He made his peace with his own, Protestant, church with many bequests, some of which are described by the ancient historian, Dugdale, thus: "Richard Lord Rich in 1564 . . . founded a free Grammer School at Felsted . . . founded almes-houses at Felsted for six poore people, and gave to be distributed to the poore of Felsted, Little Leez and Great Waltham adjoining, on severall Sundays in Lent, eleven cades of red and eleven barrells of white herrings."

For three hundred years the school continued almost exactly in the tradition of its original foundation. It was in the second half of the nineteenth century, under W. S. Grignon, that the school really grew in numbers and in reputation. Oliver Cromwell's sons went to this school, and one of them, Robert, lies by the south porch of the church, having died at the early age of eighteen. Bourchiers, back up the road across the railway, is an old farm which perpetuates the family name of Elizabeth, Cromwell's wife.

Opposite the schoolroom, on the corner, is a most interesting old house, with an inscription all along the bressumer, or main horizontal beam, which runs, "Geo. Boote built this house 1596", and that family name can be traced over hundreds of years in the registers of Felsted and Stebbing. Today the house does service as a bank during the day and a very exclusive little restaurant by night.

Stebbing church is a real discovery, made entirely of stone, which must have been brought some distance, and still completely of the fourteenth century. Its one truly remarkable feature is the rood screen, made of stone, beautifully carved in three delicate arches with further decorative subdivisions and designs. The three figures it was originally designed to support are missing, but the simple cross, or rood, from which the screen is named, still stands centrally on high. Pevsner tells us that there are only two other screens of this design in existence. One is nearby at Great Bardfield and the other, quite unaccountably is in far away Trondheim, Norway. David Howland, who lives at Church Farm, like his late father, Frank Howland before him, has collected old and beautiful objects once in daily use simply because he liked them.

David Howland made his father's dream come true, building a museum in the farmyard to house the growing and vastly interesting collections. Difficulties of security, however, forced him to sell the whole accumulation. Mr. Howland enjoys all this work but he is also a working farmer tending 200 acres which makes demands on both his time and physical energy. He works on his pastime of restoration whenever farm work allows and claims it is his way of relaxing. He has completely rebuilt a vintage car, one of several in the museum which his skill had put into working order.

The river meanders unhurriedly from Felsted to Chelmsford, and the road follows it, bend for bend, exactly at that height which kept the ancient traveller clear of winter floods. So road and river come to the Walthams, Great and Little. Not only was the Essex historian Philip Morant curate at Great Waltham, the vicar himself was Nicolas Tindal. He was there for eighteen years from 1722 and during that time he worked on a history of our county, of which one part was actually published. He was forced to give up the work through lack of support and Morant was later able to build on Tindal's firm foundation. It is his grandson Sir Nicholas Conyngham Tindal who has his effigy in Chelmsford's Tindal Square.

The "Big House" here is Langleys which first belonged to the Everard family, to one of whom, Sir Anthony, died 1609, there is a splendid monument in the church. It shows him all in alabaster, as a knight attired in full armour. The family fell on hard times and sold the estate to Samuel Tufnell in 1710. Two years later Samuel started turning the shabby old place into one of the finest houses in the county. On rare occasions it is opened to the public and one can see much of the furniture which is still contemporary with the eighteenth century tranformation: the whole place has been kept in a perfect state of preservation by the same family down to this very day. The lodge on the main road is a miniature replica, externally, of the house itself, emblazoned with the family arms.

◀ Village Street, Felsted.

Guildhall and War Memorial: Great Waltham.

The church of St Mary and St Lawrence cannot be missed because its yard makes a hairpin bend in the village street. Its strong Norman tower was strengthened in later years with great brick buttresses. Around the church there are old houses, and the ancient *Six Bells* inn, but just down the road the new small estate of ultra-modern houses has caused a good deal of controversy in the village. They more or less overlook the village war memorial, and, behind it, the Guildhall which the present Mr Tufnell recently restored. By removing the shop front the building has reverted to what it looked like in Elizabethan times, when the four beautiful twin chimney-stacks were built to crown the grand timber-framed house.

Little Waltham has an inn of but one *Bell*, as befits smaller fry. Its main street, over the recently widened Winckford Bridge, has houses of all periods in enjoyable juxtaposition and the fact that the village has been bypassed gives pedestrians the chance to walk about the place. The church is off the village centre down the lane that leads to Boreham, a Norman nave shows its age and a Perpendicular tower repaired in brick in Tudor times shows the continuing importance of its place in this little community.

The Tufnell estate also includes much of Pleshey and its castle. Not many Essex people realise that Pleshey is mentioned in Shakespeare, that this is the village where a king came riding to kill a duke, and where the villagers themselves had their revenge in the beheading of the king's conspirator-in-chief. Imagine the scene in 1397 when Richard II learned that his uncle, the Duke of Gloucester, was conspiring to oust him

118

from the throne. He invited him to Pleshey and during dinner asked him to make a diplomatic trip to Calais. There the Duke was murdered by hired assassins. When Richard was finally deposed his half-brother, prime mover in that murder plot, was taken back to the scene of his crime at Pleshey and there savagely beheaded. So, in the first act of King Richard II, the Duchess of Gloucester, in her widowed grief tells Gaunt to take her message to her brother, "Bid him—ah, what?—With all good speed at Plashy visit me."

But Pleshey's story is older than English kings. Some tribe settled in this spot in the dawn of civilisation. Labouring with tools of flint they created a mighty rampart and ditch more than a mile round. The Romans were glad to take over this ready-made fort and left their mark of habitation here. The Saxons found it all too big for them, so they built their own earthwork inside, a great moat surrounded a fifty foot high mound on which their Norman successors built their stone castle keep. The castle crumbled, but today the fifteenth century bridge across the moat is preserved as a rarity.

The modern story of this village must include T. C. Darby, who lived at Pleshey Lodge, for he was the inventor in the 1870's of the Darby steam digger which performed "spade husbandry by steam-power" at one seventh of the cost. The forge in the village at which the parts of that famous machine were made continues today in the hands of an energetic and artistic blacksmith.

West of Pleshey are the villages of Good and High Easter. Postmark collectors of an earlier day have been known to travel here from all over the country, simply to add these curiosities to their collection. The experts think the "Easter" developed from the Old English word for a sheepfold. "High" denotes the situation on higher land than "Good" which remembers a very early landowner, Godiva, widow of a wealthy Saxon.

At High Easter the church stands back, a little shy, its entrance between two old houses, gabled and timber-framed, which have guarded the path for five hundred years. One is now the Punchbowl restuarant and the other is known familiarly as "the old post-office". The church of the Virgin Mary is built of flint and rubble with later additions, like the porch and the clerestory, in Tudor brick. The impressive tower was built in the fifteenth century. On the north side, on the first pitch of the buttress you will see the imprint of a hand, which is said by some to be the mark of the Devil, and by others to be a rough memorial by his fellows to a workman who fell to his death during the construction of that tower.

The rather splendid tomb to Dame Agnes Gates has been a casualty of time, but there are many reminders of the past to be seen in a perambulation of the place. The sedilia, the piscina, the three-hundred-year-old chair, the font which is nearly twice as old, and the large parish chest which is about five hundred years old. The last-named bears evidence that it was violently forced open about three hundred years ago. That needed some strength, for it was iron bound, with seven different locks.

The blacksmith's house still stands, along the village street. When the last blacksmith laid his hammer on the anvil for the last time the place stayed exactly as he had left it for close on twenty-five years. When Christopher Coe came here as village blacksmith in 1906, he was continuing a family craft already a century old, and that craft died when illness forced him to give up in 1949. But instead of the decay, damage and loss which is usually the fate of the old craftsmen's tools and premises the High Easter forge has been fully measured and photographed and the tools bought in their entirety at a nominal price by the Chelmsford and Essex Museum from the blacksmith's son, Eric Coe, who felt that such preservation would serve two purposes. It would show people yet unborn what a blacksmith's shop was like in the early twentieth century, with all the tools he used, and it would be a fitting memorial to the life-work of his father, and a long line of Essex craftsmen whose way of life has disappeared.

The shop and Post Office: High Easter.

Another village craft persisted on the other side of the road. The Bircher brothers continued as village grocers with a clientele which appreciated individual service from people who had learned their knowledge over many years. What could not be obtained from their general stores and post office was not worth having. Derek Bircher is also responsible for the published history of this interesting village for he has written *One village in history; being an account of the history of High Easter in Essex*. In 112 close-packed pages this villager, proud of his village, has covered every aspect of its story.

The life-giving water of the River Roding was the reason for the settlements on its banks all the way down to Barking and the Thames. In this area there are eight such settlements which include the river's name in their titles. Let us start in the north with High Roding, so called from its loftier situation above the river. Its village street offers a pleasant view, a real advertisement for all the charm and homeliness of village life. The *Lamb* at one end of the street and the *Black Bull*, a plastered, timber-framed building, at the other remind us that travellers have been glad to put up for the night.

120

On the way to Leaden Roding there is a tiny lane off on the right which leads past High Rodingbury to the church of All Saints, to peter out at the edge of a field. At that very point the church is an invitation into village history, but its distance from habitation and the increase of petty damage has caused the key to be kept at the Rectory at Leaden Roding. Inside, the furnishings are as simple and honest as the faith which has been demonstrated here since its erection at the end of the twelfth century.

The pulpit is a delight to the eye, a Jacobean gem, beautifully constructed and carved in wood, it swells out from a central stem. By the organ, near the tiny vestry there is a brass inscription on the floor which catches the eye, and the imagination.

"John Jocelyn, esquire, interred here doth lie,
Sir Thomas Jocelyn's third son of worthy memory.
Thrice noble was this gentleman by birth, by learning great,
By single chast and godly life, he won in heaven a seate;
He the year one thousand and five hundred twentynine was born,
Not twenty yeares old him Cambridge did with two degrees adorn.
King's College him a fellow chose, in anno forty-nine,
In learning tryde whereto he did his mind alwaies incline,
But others took the praise and fame of his deserving wit,
And his inventions as their own, to printing did commit.
One thousand six hundred and three it grieves all to remember,
He left this life (poor's daily friend), the twentyeighth December."

It is tempting to read into the third and fourth to last lines a clue to another claimant in the "Who wrote Shakespeare?" controversy. The Jocelynes lived in New Hall, a mile due west of the church on the other side of the Roding, which they built in the seventeenth century on an old moated site.

Outside, All Saints' appearance was considerably altered in May 1832 when, according to the *Kent and Essex Mercury*, "On the 15th instant, the spire of High Roothing church was struck by lightning; being composed of wood it was set on fire, and but for great exertions, the whole fabric might have been reduced to a state of ruin." So the very graceful spire had to be replaced by the best that could then be afforded, in the shape of a small bell turret which still exists.

Down the lane there is the driveway to High Rodingbury. A "Bury" denoted the site of a manor house in Saxon times, and any visitor to the house today will not be disappointed by the view. Though it has been demoted from the status of the Hall of the Saxon chief to a mere farmhouse today, the plaster front, the Georgian doorway, the little windows and the moat still filled with water all tell the story of its being lived in over hundreds of years, and through the range of vicissitudes which time inevitably brings.

From here the B184 passes through Aythorpe Roding with its delightful windmill to Leaden Roding, so called, it is believed, because it had the first church hereabouts to be roofed with lead. White Roding is further along the busy A414, but the church can be found down a quiet lane, where the sturdy sixteenth century tower thrusts up through the trees a tall spire which is a landmark for miles. It was the light-coloured rubble walls of that church which gave the settlement that "white" appellation. There are a number of interesting features to be seen within.

A quarter of a mile further down the lane stands the village windmill. Once the flour factory for the whole area it lost its custom to the steam machines of the Victorian age and mouldered to a shadow of its former glory, when it was lucky enough to find a sympathetic owner who virtually rebuilt it. The lane wanders on past Mascallsbury, an ancient moated building, to Abbess Roding and past its church to Rookwood Hall. The old house on this site was built in 1523 and visited on three occasions by Queen Elizabeth I. Its owner, Wistan Browne, was father of Sir Antony Browne, founder of Brentwood School.

Take the next left turn off the A414 and there is what appears to be a mighty tumulus, a great mound raised as the burial chamber of an ancient British chief. Do not be misled, it was raised to make targets for the Americans on the airfield there to test their guns in the last war.

Abbess, Beauchamp and Berners Roding are run together these days as a civil parish. Here two people should be remembered, separated though they are by six centuries. The first is Dame Juliana Berners, whose family gave the village its name. She was the daughter of Sir James Berners who was executed in 1388 for his loyalty to Richard II. She grew up in this wild and beautiful river valley and went to court knowing the arts of hunting, hawking and fishing, which were then much in vogue as royal pursuits. When she grew older she took holy orders and became Prioress of a nunnery at Sopwell. There, in her spare time she compiled a book on those pursuits and combined with them a treatise on heraldry with the general title, "Treatyse perteynynge to Hawkynge, Huntynge, Fysshynge and Coote Armiris". It achieved fame as one of the very first books to be printed in this country, as far back as 1481.

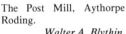

The Post Mill, Aythorpe Roding.

Walter A. Blythin

122

The second person is a man of the twentieth century. On a side road off the B184, which runs from Leaden Roding down to Beauchamp Roding there is a drive to what was once Hornets Farm, now amalgamated in a bigger estate. Beside that drive, among the nettles and the brambles you can see the graves of a farmer and his wife, and two of their sons, the last buried only recently. Those tombstones tell a story.

Isaac Mead was an independent small farmer who came up the hard way, a humble labourer for years before he could borrow enough money to risk on a small place of his own. It was his passion to be his own master, to make his life wholly dependant on his own efforts. He succeeded, and, when he was near to dying, he had part of one of his fields consecrated so that he and his family might find eternal rest in a corner of the land which had succoured them in life. Isaac was born on 23rd January 1859 at the Building Yard, High Easter. His earliest memory was of the wedding of the Prince of Wales in 1863, when the village celebrated with a big procession and tea for everyone in the barn.

He never realised how poor his parents were until he overhead them talking, trying to decide whether to buy boots for their boys, or pay the weekly "club" which would be their only income if father fell ill. Isaac, nine years old, slipped out of the cottage that very night and ran to the bailiff of Bury Farm, where he fixed up to start work the following Monday. His parents when they heard of it were proud, but adamant; he was to stay at school. Before he was eleven, however, he had a job looking after sheep and filling in time weeding and cutting thistles, all for one and sixpence a week. This went up to two and sixpence when he was entrusted with milking the cows six days a week. One morning he climbed an oak tree to help shake out the acorns, slipped and fell twenty-five feet into a ditch, breaking his thigh. Medical treatment a hundred years ago can hardly be imagined, but the country doctor was a devoted man. After eight weeks in a splint the boy was told he could sit outside without it. He did so, moved awkwardly, fainted with the pain, fell from the chair and broke that thigh again. After months of recuperation, Isaac, still but thirteen years old, was ready for work again on Heron's Farm, High Easter. In 1874 the fifteen year old had his first swing of a scythe when the working day for a labourer in the harvest field was from 5 a.m. to 7 p.m. and a countryman had to be very tough.

Fate led Isaac on to a windmill at seventeen, where he learned to dress the stones and keep the mill in full working order. The next year, when a mighty gale sprang up he saved the mill by his quickness and commonsense, whereas the White Roding mill, six miles away, threw a sail and was blown over. On visits home, Isaac had met a young lady and now they were courting strongly. It made him determine to strike out on his own. He saw an advertisement for the renting of Waples Mill Farm, which lies by the Roding on the lane from Margaret Roding to Berners Roding. In 1882 he borrowed £200, married and went straight into the almost derelict farm. The debt was cleared and other commitments came, in the shape of four hungry sons to be fed off the farm profits. Through these years Isaac Mead did what he could to further the work of the Parish Council when it came into being following the 1893 Act. His own struggles on the land made him the right person to negotiate for allotments for the villagers.

Isaac Mead and his family
in the harvest field, 1896.

With his sons growing and helping, the farm slowly improved and Isaac introduced new ideas. Hornets Farm was rented as the family expanded its little empire. We know all this and much more because in 1922 he had a nasty accident and during recovery time hung heavily, so he decided to "put a few of the pitfalls encountered during my career on record for the benefit of others." This little book, *The Life Story of an Essex Lad*, now only available in libraries, is a collector's item, which gives a picture of Essex farming life over a period of seventy years. It is a monument to the very hard work of an ordinary Essex farm labourer who succeeded in his efforts to have his own farm, to the degree that he was once entertained by the late Sir Winston Churchill for his views on the de-rating of agricultural property. All that remains of that effort are those tombstones and that book and one simple saying of Isaac Mead's that shall be his epitaph, "My sympathies have always been with men of all classes who try to leave the world better than they found it."

From the Rodings there is a pleasant country lane from Fyfield to Roxwell and the A414 near Chelmsford. It covers about eight miles, and hundreds of years of Essex history. Willingale lies halfway along that road, the centre of a spider's web of country lanes. The visitor is surprised to see two fine churches in one churchyard in such a small village. That is because it is really two quite separate places; Willingale Doe and Willlingale Spain. They crown the high ground overlooking the vale of the Roding to the west, which makes a beautiful view from various points in the village, but particularly at the end of the churchyard. Their names help to tell much of their story.

Willingale: two churches in one churchyard.   ▶

Willingale is a slurring over the centuries of Willinghall, shown in the Domesday Book as Willinghala, which indicates the headquarters of a Saxon chief. The "Doe" and the "Spain" take the story on through Norman times, for two of William the Conqueror's trusty knights were rewarded for their services with all the land hereabout. Their names were William de Ou and Hervey de Ispania and a version of those names continues to differentiate the two settlements, though they are now so fused that it would be hard to decipher their original boundaries and their churches stand next to each other. Such an unusual situation has brought forth all kinds of local legend in explanation. One of the most popular stories is recounted by Coller in his *People's History of Essex* based on his visit to Willingale in the 1820's where he was told that the whole of the village lands were held by two sisters, who fell out one day about where they sat in their pew. One sister determined never to sit near the other again, so, being very rich, she built her own church next door, thus ensuring her own pew and position in it.

The older church of St Andrew's is now closed for worship. Its nave was built in the twelfth century using some Roman bricks. The belfry, made for two bells, spans the nave with its massive timber, showing the builder's art in bringing just the right-shaped timbers straight from the forest to joint and peg into a frame which has taken the weight of those swinging bells through half a millenium. This church is noted for two curiosities; the strange old doorways, made of very thin Roman tiles, and the door itself which is almost covered in wrought iron work. St Christopher's has recently been the subject of careful restoration under the guidance of the Reverend George Marsden, who has been at great pains to see that certain monuments, moved in the past without reference to their original positions, are put back in their correct places, as far as can be ascertained from the records now available. So some amends are being made for the drastic restoration of 1853. There are interesting brasses here from that to Thomas Torell of 1442 down to various members of the Wiseman family two centuries later. The stone walls and the big square embattled tower of stone, rebuilt in 1853, make the difference between the two churches very obvious.

On the other side of the road stands one of the two village inns, the *Bell*. The previous old landlord, of pleasant memory, chuckled as he told me the little joke he must have cracked a thousand times to sightseers; "There you are," he said, "two churches—and only one Bell between them." The Bramston family were once connected with the Rectory and included the great house of Skreens at Roxwell among their property. It is now just an outline of foundations in the fields off to the right on the road through Shellow Bowells, where the old brick church, built in 1754 is now disused and looking for a sympathetic owner. Surely, in Shellow Bowells, Essex can claim one of the most curious place names in the country. It has been assembled from an old English word for a winding river and the family name of Lambert de Buella, itself a derivation from the French place name Bouelles.

The next village along the lane has another of those intriguing names, Roxwell. It signifies the settlement by a Saxon tribe under the leadership of Hroc beside a stream, or well which was one of the essential elements in any choice of living place. The well still flows in a pond in the village street beside which the *Chequers* shows its eighteenth century facade and next to it the old clapboard and tile building which housed the general stores and village café. This was run by the late Mrs Olive Brewer who catered for village hall events for miles around. Around the corner, in the new vicarage, lived until recently the Reverend Philip Wright. He is known nationally for his knowledge of horses, has written *Salute the Carthorse* which brings back the memory of what the horse meant to man before mechanisation on the farm. The vicar has moved with the times, however, and is also an authority on traction engines and tractors, on which he has also written books. He writes with authority on farming matters in the county magazine.

The village shop and pub, Roxwell.

CHAPTER TEN

Setting Out from Stock for the Dengie Peninsula

FROM the southern outskirts of Chelmsford the B1007 crosses Galleywood Common on its way to the pretty village of Stock. The days of the horse races on the Common are still remembered, for, although they began in the eighteenth century, when George III gave a special prize for one of the races, they were revived in this century, until the course was sold just before the last war. Its outline can still be detected as it runs in a big oval round the church and across the main road.

Stock should really be called Stock Harvard as it was in the fourteenth century, showing that in Saxon times it was still showing the stumps, or stocks of the trees of a newly cleared part of the forest belonging to the Hereward or Steward. That Steward may well have been Sir Thomas Tyrell, Earl of Essex, who was held responsible for the death of William Rufus in the New Forest in 1100. In those early days Stock is thought to have been but a hamlet of Buttsbury, now only a hamlet itself, which then rejoiced in the name of Gyngjoyeberdlaundrey.

All Saints church, Stock.   *Walter A. Blythin*

East of Stock lies a great stretch of water, the Hanningfield reservoir, 874 acres of water, costing over £6,000,000 to confine it and a vital source of water supply in south east Essex. Much of the water actually comes from Langford, as we have noted under that village. In the early days the flies that bred on this still water became a nuisance to the villagers on the brink. So the water engineers stocked the reservoir with fish, they ate the flies, and the water authority issued licences, at no small cost, for people to come and catch the well-fed fish. So a nice little ecological circle solved the problem.

At Rettendon the church is lofty, windblown and 158 feet above the creek of the Crouch which runs under the mill at nearby Battlesbridge. From its tower it is possible to see out over the North Sea and from the church yard the view landwards is impressive. Inside is the sumptuous monument to Edward Humphrey, last of his line, who died in 1727. It is thirty feet high, includes five figures in its allegory and is carried out in a number of Italian marbles.

At the moment the new township of South Woodham Ferrers is taking shape. Houses, schools, shops, offices and workplaces have risen all round the old village centre. The reason for this "town in the country" is best summed up by the County Council in its Handbook: "Pressure for housing in Essex continues today as it has done for several centuries. As the existing towns grow larger there is a growing demand to provide homes in the green belt and agricultural landscape of the County. As a positive contribution the County Council as planning authority decided that South Woodham Ferrers constituted an area where housing could be provided without materially restricting the availability of open space for amenity and re-creation."

The present population of some 4,000 will rise to a projected 18,000. I like the housing policy which provides " . . . a variety of housing in accordance with the County Council's 'Design Guide' for residential areas to satisfy the needs of those coming into the area . . . " including " . . . very small dwellings in line with a national trend towards smaller households allowing more owner occupation for those in the lower income bracket," and the fact that, "Development by housing associations providing homes for the elderly or other special categories is being considered in an attempt to provide a balanced community . . . It is desirable that young and old should live together and seek satisfaction in working for each other."

Shops are situated in a town centre which also boasts a comprehensive, "service centre" for the whole community, including school, sports centre, community centre, church and the various local government and professional services. So just for a change here is a place which is turning its back on its past to spend the present planning a really pleasant and rewarding environment for its citizens of the future.

Looking eastwards, Purleigh should be mentioned because no less a person than the great-great-grandfather of George Washington was rector here in 1633. Because this Laurence Washington had royalist sympathies he was ejected from his living in 1643. He later held a curacy at Little Braxted and was eventually buried in All Saints church at Maldon.

Turn to the Essex County Handbook and you will find a brief entry for Southminster, "Small market town between the Crouch and Blackwater and the terminus of a branch railway from Wickford. Large church with work of many

In the fields near Purleigh: a woman drives the combine harvester.

periods. Between the town and the North Sea are the extensive and lonely areas of the Dengie Marshes." But the Dengie peninsula merits more than a sentence. In fact there is one man who has written many thousands of words about the people who dwell in these remote flatlands. Samuel Levy Bensusan, born in 1872, came to Essex around 1908. It is said that while working as a journalist in London he became ill and was ordered by his doctor to recover in the bracing air of the Essex coast. At that time he was editor of the *Jewish World* and had been music critic for the *Illustrated London News, The Sketch* and *Vanity Fair*. He had also written books on faraway places in which he had wandered at the turn of the century.

Now he applied his interest and his wonderfully descriptive and evocative style to this area of Essex and put together stories of " . . . the most homely scenes still unchronicled in England, aspiring to do for the Essex marshes something of what Hardy did for Dorset." He started with *A Countryside Chronicle* and continued with *Marshland Voices, Annals of Maychester, Marshland Calling*, and so the stream flowed on. In reviewing his *A Marshland Omnibus* in 1954 the *Essex County Standard* said, "Mr Bensusan's 60 years of living observantly and imaginatively in these parts and among its people have yielded 60 books, together with innumerable hundred short stories, essays and talks . . . The way of life described in his writing is, as he recognises, much changed in Marshland nowadays, though the underlying motives, the essential backgrounds and the eternal rhythms are possibly less altered than we may sometimes fear . . . During many years he made extensive tours on agricultural affairs, broadcast often, ran two small farms and watched through wars and peace the passing of the last peasants, the vernacular speech, the immemorial ways, the coming of recompenses he deems spurious." He lived in the heart of the Dengie peninsula, at Asheldam, and later at Mote Cottage between St Lawrence and Bradwell-juxta-Mare. Eventually he removed to Godfreys at Langham, near Colchester, but not before he had amassed a store of observations of life in the land of marsh and salting. By the time he died in December 1958 his stories had brought rural Essex before the world.

The change in the area is best reflected at Bradwell, as explained by the old Rural District's guide: " . . . one of the oldest existing Christian churches in England still stands beside the shore where it was built in the 7th century. Yet within two miles of this most ancient place and the Roman fort upon the site of which it was erected, is the great atomic power station which has been built by the Central Electricity Authority . . . " The brooding bulk of that huge building is a landmark seen for miles across the Dengie flats and the hum of its turbines is felt as much as heard. In the shadow of the power station yachts and motor boats are launched from the slipway which runs out between Pewet Island and Bradwell's sea wall into the Blackwater estuary.

The old village of Bradwell is further south and off the B1021; in connection with which it is apposite to mention that Sir Henry Bate-Dudley who lived in the house now called Bradwell Lodge. He had it extended in tasteful style by John Johnson, the well-known architect who designed Chelmsford's Shire Hall. Henry, born in 1745, grew up to be a real Essex "character" for he combined parson, magistrate, sportsman and editor of the *Morning Post* all in his one expansive person. He liked to travel frequently to town but hated the roughness of the ride occasioned by awful roads. He did not just complain about it; he set to work and spent more than £28,000 in and about Bradwell on improving roads and land generally by extensive draining which reclaimed for use more than 250 acres of marshland. He made a name for himself as a huntsman by being the only man in at the kill on the roof of Cricksea church where the fox was followed up an ivy-covered buttress by Sir Henry and half a dozen hounds. Bradwell Lodge, with its unusual belvedere on the roof and rooms which show the work of Robert Adam and Angelica Kauffmann has more recently been lived in by the late Tom Driberg, M.P.

Bradwell Lodge.

Walter A. Blythin

St Peter on the Wall, Bradwell.   *Owen Keen*

   The church nearby has a fourteenth century nave and chancel which was much restored in 1864, and a stout brick tower put up in 1706, but the appeal of St Thomas's to the visitor is over-shadowed by the simple, barn-like building which stands on the sea wall a mile and a half to the northeast, at the end of a track which was obviously a Roman road. Nikolaus Pevsner maintains, "It is in all probability the very church built by St Cedd c.654." If that is the case only the nave now remains and for many years in this century that had served as a barn for a local farmer until interest was aroused in the amazing story of its origin as that first Saxon church known all down the years as the Chapel of St Peter ad Murum—St Peter on the Wall. Excavation has shown that an apse at the east end extended seventeen feet further towards the sea, perched on the foundations of the Roman fort which preceded it by about five hundred years. Its tower was still standing at the end of the eighteenth century but by then maps were marking it as "now a barn" and it was not until 22nd June 1920 that, through the generosity of an anonymous Essex man, who paid for the work required to make it structurally sound while adding nothing that could hint at restoration, it was at last re-consecrated by the first Bishop of Chelmsford. His successors have since then made it the subject of an annual pilgrimage.
   Tillingham, like Bradwell, sits well inland behinds its flats where Marshhouse Decoy Pond reminds us how duck were caught in their hundreds in these marshes to provide the tables of the London rich with a tasty morsel. The village street is something of a fraud; the many typically Essex weatherboarded cottages give a really ancient atmosphere, but many of them were built, in the old style, around 1880 by the lord of the manor—no less a body than the Dean and Chapter of St Paul's, who

131

received the manor and tithes as early as the sixth century from Ethelbert. The church of St Nicholas was given a new south aisle in 1866 and a complete restoration in 1891. The chiming clock was installed in the battlemented twelfth century tower in 1887, Queen Victoria's Golden Jubilee. The old village lock-up or cage still stands in the shadow of that tower. Local miscreants were incarcerated there until the constable could make arrangements to have them taken to Maldon or Chelmsford to answer for their crime.

Asheldham is as important for what is under the land as for what is on it, and the gravel deposits around it have been extensively worked. The origin of the name is lost in the same antiquity which cloaks the meaning of the two sets of earthworks which can still faintly be detected. One encloses the church, the hall and the pond, the other takes in a larger area altogether and has not been satisfactorily explained. The church of St Lawrence, now converted for use as a youth centre, has a strong tower some six hundred years old whose battlemented top has been restored in brick, making it an easily recognizable landmark.

Dengie gives its name to the whole Hundred of parishes and yet appears quite insignificant upon the map east of Asheldham, south of Tillingham and lining a lane which goes nowhere in particular because the only access to the sea wall eastwards is the drive to the Grange and a subsequent footpath. Even when standing on the sea wall one can still see the mud flats stretching out more than a mile to the broad blue band of a North Sea horizon.

Southminster is further inland again, behind the Dengie marshes watered by the Asheldam Brook and a thousand others springs and drains which run either seawards or to the Crouch on the southern side. Here you can say you are in a town, for it still has its own market. Its isolation, its country way of life was doomed when the railway crept in from Wickford. Now new estates have been developed and the centre of the town is in process of change with empty shops, demolition sites, new buildings and old pubs and houses all mixed up in an interim period. In the old church of St Leonard there is evidence in its construction of Norman origin, though it is largely of fifteenth century work, which in itself has been spoiled by unsympathetic restorations in the eighteenth and nineteenth centuries. The intriguing feature here is the fact that Dr Alexander Scott, Vicar from 1809 to 1840, was a great friend of Nelson, acting as his secretary and his chaplain. He sailed with him to the Mediterranean theatre of war in 1803 and was at the end, the man in whose arms he died on the *Victory*. From that famous ship Scott brought Nelson's chart table, bureau and mirror and installed them in the vestry of this church where they can been seen today.

Scott was also curate at Burnham-on-Crouch around 1809. There the connection ends, for while Southminster may have lessened in importance as a market town in the marshes, Burnham has advanced as a famous yachting centre whose week of racing is second socially only to that of Cowes. The old Urban District Council guide has an other-worldliness about it.: "If you can't manage without noisy fun-fairs, or clacking pin-tables or persistent beach photographers or concert parties, then our town isn't for you. If, however, you have a yearning for quietness, for pleasant country walks and equally pleasant drives, for watching small boats dancing on dappled water or 'mucking about in small boats' yourself, for the kind of peace that seeps right into your mind, then decidedly Burnham-on-Crouch is the place for you."

The fact that Burnham has no through traffic, combined with its position on the bank of the Crouch as it widens to its estuary adds to its attraction. The long, straight quay backed by boatyards, houses, restaurants, inns—of all ages and architecture, is perfect for a morning stroll. Behind the quay is the High Street, one of the widest in Essex, with its very distinctive clock tower put up in 1877. It was the subject of an improvement scheme by the Civic Trust in 1963 which very successfully harmonised old and new. From here back up to the station are all the shops and an increasing number of houses in roads which on the map point like a finger post to St Mary's church on the very outskirts of the present town. It is old, and storms blew down the tower in 1703 and the spire in 1779. A fire in 1774 destroyed the roof of the nave and just one of the registers, covering marriages 1754 to 1774 which could have been left out in the church for a marriage which was about to take place. There have been patient rebuildings after each catastrophe and constant restorations of the ravages of time itself.

The Baptists in Burnham can claim one of the oldest congregations in the country. At their chapel in Station Road are records which date from 1673, just one year after Charles II's royal decree that nonconformists would be allowed to build their own places of worship. But if there is any building which enshrines the spirit of Burnham it must be the headquarters of the Royal Corinthian Yacht Club, seawards down the river. There is nothing old about this white, ferro-concrete, three-storeyed building which from a distance seems to float on the water. It was designed in 1931 by Joseph Emberton and won him an award from the *Daily Express*. In this club and in the Royal Burnham, the Crouch and other yacht and sailing clubs up and down the quay the personalities will be found—characters and stories needing a separate book as they range from national figures like Ted Heath and his *Morning Cloud* to the tyro and his pram dinghy.

Despite this important and constant use of the river it is only now that ownership of it and a large part of the estuary is being sorted out. In March 1978 the *Daily Telegraph* reported that the Crouch Harbour Authority was considering buying a seven-mile stretch of the Crouch from the Burnham River Company, which maintained that it owned freehold rights granted even before Magna Carta to the Lord of the Manor of Burnham, from whom the rights were purchased by local oyster merchants and thus acquired by the Whitstable oystermen who set up the Company here in 1953. This Company has been the subject of take-over bids which have raised the value, influenced perhaps by the possibility of the new airport at Maplin, from £11,897 before take-over to its sale to the Industrial Midlands Investment Trust for £200,000. Yet the company had but 30,000 brood oysters in one of its three oyster beds and only one oyster dredging boat. Oysters cannot be bred in the Crouch today so they have to be bought in and left in the beds to mature for two summers. The other asset claimed by the Company was the control of the moorings but a bill promoted in Parliament to establish this failed and the Crouch Harbour Authority was formed to take control of the river in April 1975. That Authority acquired these ancient rights later in 1978.

The B1010 in its progress to Althorne roughly parallels the bank of the Crouch, passing by Creeksea with its tall church tower, rebuilt by Frederick Chancellor, first Mayor of Chelmsford and architect of local note, just a hundred years ago. In the new building a brass of 1631 was retained celebrating Sir Arthur Harris. He lived at Creeksea Place down by the Crouch when it was still a big Tudor mansion built in 1569. The Mildmays acquired it in 1652 and later owners demolished the south and east wings and removed them to London. William Rome of Burnham, who died in 1907, built the house now standing on the foundations of the east wing, but there is still Elizabethan work surviving in the north range of buildings.

The fact that the Essex Farmers Hunt has its kennels in the next parish, Althorne, may well have given rise to the name of the public house which stands so picturesquely just off the B1010 on the lane to Southminster. It is called the *Huntsman and Hounds* and I mention it because at the time of writing it approaches as nearly to the traditional Essex village inn as any I have discovered. The scrubbed deal tables, the benches, the small bar counter with barrels on view behind it, the cheerful landlord and his lady all combine to produce an atmosphere in which everybody can and does join in friendly conversation.

The Huntsman and Hounds: Althorne.

From the church of St Andrew the parish stretches south to include the station, and beyond it, Bridgemarsh Island, a marshy fen formed by the meandering Crouch.

Immediately north of Althorne is Mayland, a parish in which development has switched from the village centre at Mayland where the church of St Barnabas was rebuilt in 1867, through Lower Mayland on the road to Steeple and Bradwell and up to Maylandsea which has considerably expanded in recent years. Now the authorities are concerned to improve conditions in this growing settlement and a Mayland Village Plan has been prepared to see that all the amenities are provided. One of the difficulties encountered has been the number of un-made roads and lack of services to the many smallholdings established here. From these independent, hard-working people who built their own houses and wrenched a living from a few acres of soil let me pick one personality.

The fact that Mayland became an area of smallholdings and nursery gardens is due to the influence of Joseph Fels, a rich American who was totally opposed to the ownership of land by a few wealthy people. He bought up a lot of land in this country, some of it here in Mayland, and split it up among smallholders who were united in a co-operative venture under a manager paid by Fels to show them how to grow and sell their crops successfully. The manager he chose was Thomas Smith. After a long career in printing, and having been his own master in a small business for seventeen years since his marriage in 1879, Thomas decided to give it all up and go in for the quiet life in horticulture. It is thought that he was influenced by articles in *The Clarion* in 1896 about the success of a smallholder who was making a go of it on just three acres of Essex soil.

So that was where he went. Having sold his business for £800, he bought eleven acres of land at Mayland, built a house on it and called it "The Homestead". On these acres, five of pasture and six of weed covered and wet arable, he tried cows, pigs and poultry, but they did not pay the bills. For six months, as long as his wife could manage on her own, he worked as a printer in Manchester to pay his way. Then through a mortgage from a lawyer friend he was able to change his set-up into fruit and kitchen crops. The locals were not helpful but Thomas took any kind of odd job to help out and gradually the enterprise prospered and he had saved enough to build two 50 by 20 feet glasshouses for tomatoes and cucumbers. These he discovered were the right kind of crops for an Essex smallholding, so cows and chicken were sold off and more glasshouses built to bring in crops like lettuce and early strawberries.

It was at this point that he felt able to offer himself to Mr Fels as manager of the co-operative set up so near The Homestead. It gave him the chance to study the French gardening system of intensive cultivation which was the natural extension of his own glasshouse practice. The two of them went to Paris to see the system in operation and they engaged a French grower to come back to Mayland with his family and he taught Thomas a number of new practices. Smith then wrote a book, *French Gardening* which was published in 1909. It was a carefully written book in which he stated honestly that he had no financial interest; he simply wished to answer as well as he could the many enquiries he received as manager of this unusual horticultural system. He warned smallholders with a good reserve of capital to go carefully, but pointed out that from Mayland they were able to send to Covent Garden salad crops, early vegetables and Cantaloupe melons which attracted higher prices than the much-vaunted foreign produce. Thomas applied common sense to the subject; "Many people actually think that by reading a book and getting a few verbal explanations they can forthwith undertake, without further preliminary, this highly specialist business, with full expectation of making a living. Such expectation is foolish and must end in disappointment and disaster." He had seen too many hard times himself to misrepresent the facts and he still had problems. The *maraîcher*, the

Frenchman brought over to run the French garden said his wife was homesick, so Thomas dug deep in his pocket and sent them both on holiday in France for a fortnight with all expenses paid. They never came back; he found later that they had gone to a better-paid job at Brighton. But the last, unsurmountable problem was the First World War which denied him both labour and a supply of manure. The French garden had to be given up.

He continued management of the smallholdings and branched out into lecturing on horticulture. The thought struck him that his lecture notes would form the basis of a useful book. Because of his previous experience in the trade he determined to print it himself. He invested £250 in the necessary equipment, just enough to set up four pages at a time, and after beginning by writing it out first in longhand he went on to set the book in type straight from his thoughts. When he had finished he had a book already set up and as Thomas said, "I don't suppose there was ever an author who went in search of a publisher with his book already set up and with the plates all ready for the press." His book, *The Profitable Culture of Vegetables*, for market gardeners, smallholders and others, was published in 1911 by Longmans and through many years and several revisions became a classic on gardening.

Many well-known people came to Mayland to see the working of the co-operative and to meet its author-manager; they included Rider Haggard, Sidney and Beatrice Webb, Keir Hardie, Prince Kropotkin, and George Lansbury. Sad to say, the co-operative began to fail, largely through petty dishonesty. The quality of the produce sent to London was spoiled by "topping-up" by some members, so it was decided to sell as much as possible in the locality to get better returns. Three horse-drawn lorries were bought to deliver in three segments of a district all around Mayland. But systematic thieving from the lorries at night was so serious, and so difficult to check that the scheme had to be closed down. Even the workers in the fields were stealing part of the produce they were gathering and selling it for their own benefit. Joseph Fels had continued to make constant visits to the projects but in the face of such subversion he became disillusioned and sold off many of the small holdings. Thomas Smith returned to The Homestead which he continued to manage himself until he was seventy-five. His wife died in 1939 but he lived on until 1955 when he died aged 98. In 1950, very late in life, he was awarded a Veitch Memorial gold medal by the Royal Horticultural Society, " . . . in recognition of the work you have done for horticulture and in particular as the author of that magnificent text-book *The Profitable Culture of Vegetables.*

My attention was drawn to this interesting character by Ronald Webber in his *Early Horticulturists* (1968), which concludes that . . . "*The Profitable Culture of Vegetables* remains to this day a classic of commercial horticulture and certainly the only gardening book to have been 'Written' and set up in type in a potting shed."

Peter Pan playground: Southend.
Owen Keen ▶

CHAPTER ELEVEN

Between the Thames and the Crouch

SOUTHEND-ON-SEA—Queen of the Essex Coast! A queen who grew up so quickly yet so successfully that she has been courted by faithful followers all through the years. It all started in Prittlewell with the building in 1767 of a few extra red brick cottages called Pleasant Row, where people from London could rent a cottage or have board and lodging for a holiday in the relaxing air where the Thames broadens out to the North Sea. The rapid development of the place in keeping up with what the public wanted for the perfect holiday could hardly have been foreseen, yet it was by one man. The Reverend Thomas Archer was approaching middle age in 1794 when he wrote *A Poetical Description of New South-End*. Just twenty-five years after that first terrace was built he already saw the possibilities.

He foresaw the streets extended and buildings rise in a new South-End where Londonders would flock away from the smoke into the purer air. He also envisaged the noise of visitors making their way there, the peace of the cliff-side gardens which led down to the beach. Any visitor to Southend today can descend through the cliff gardens above Marine Parade, where the sandy beach is preceded by fairy tale characters larger than life picked out in all the glory of coloured lights at night, and a Peter Pan playground which offers noisy fun for children. The reverend gentleman might be surprised to see the dolphins giving their uncomfortably intelligent performance every hour in the old swimming pool a little further along. The spendid new swimming pool is in Warrior Square, up in the town. The pier, obviously the most prominent feature of the coast, is worthy of civic pride as the longest in the world; but it was badly damaged by fire in July 1976 and the cost of its rebuilding leaves a question mark hanging over its future. For something like fifty years it has been a phenomenon—a landing stage for steamers, a theatre, an exhibition hall, an amusement arcade, a restuarant and acres of space for promenading—all of it a mile and a quarter out to sea. Let us hope that it can be reconstructed.

Since Southend-on-Sea was, until local government reorganisation in 1974, the only county borough in Essex of which it was by far the largest town with a population of around 170,000, and because it is far and away the most popular place in the county for holidaymakers and day-trippers it follows that it deserves a coverage which cannot be afforded in a book which aims to roam all round the county. There is a coach park that can accommodate 500 coaches and car parking is available in multi-storey parks and up and down the Parades and Esplanades which cover seven miles of waterfront. The Kursaal, past the pier and the boating pool, offers endless amusement of the mechanical kind though the Big Dipper no longer operates, while, on the other side of the promenade, the sands seem to stretch away for ever at low tide—wonderful walking for adults and paddling for children and, let's face it, a good many grandparents as well.

Up in the centre of town there is the Big Top pedestrian precinct stretching down to the old main street and built up on several levels. Here again there is excitement in the noise and bustle of holiday shopping, wining and dining or just watching the world go by. There are quiet places too, like the Beecroft Art Gallery on the corner of Station Road and Westcliff Avenue which is free to all and shows eight galleries of British and European art. Priory Park is a haven of peace with beautiful flowers and shrubs surrounding the Museum in the old Prittlewell Priory, or rather, what remains of it, largely the refectory and the west range of the cloister where a fifteenth century roof survives. Excavations have revealed much of the extent of this Cluniac Benedictine cell of the chief House at Lewes, and the foundations have been marked in the turf. A modern wing houses the South East Essex Museum of Life from Stone Age to Steam Age. Nearby you will see the Crowstone, a stone obelisk which once stood on the foreshore at Chalkwell to mark the eastern limit of the City of London's authority over the Thames and its traffic.

A good account of buildings old and new to be remarked in the town itself and in all those villages from Old Leigh in the west to Shoeburyness in the east which were brought into the County Borough since its inception in 1914 can be had in Nikolaus Pevsner's *Essex* in the Penguin Buildings of England series. It includes the old, like Southchurch Hall, a fourteenth and sixteenth century timber-framed manor house with Tudor additions in which a museum has recently been established, including a reproduction of a late medieval open-hall setting, standing in a beautiful garden enhanced by the series of pools formed from the old moat. The Cliffs Pavilion is Southend's premier centre for entertainment with star shows, celebrity concerts, pop groups and dances, boxing and wrestling, pantomime, flower festivals and many other things.

People have found this south-east corner of Essex hospitable ever since the Danish chieftain Hasten beached his boats at South Shoebury and threw up the earthworks of a camp now buried beneath the barracks built by the Anglo-Saxons of our age to discourage just such another invasion. At the other end of the Borough the long, narrow creek which runs from the quay at Old Leigh out into the stream was used as a naval base by Admiral Blake when fitting out his fleet in the seventeenth century. Shortly after 1700 the shallows from here right down to Southchurch were gradually taken up as oyster beds. Then the late eighteenth century fashion for sea bathing brought the building of homes and a hotel or two, like the *Ship* in Marine

Parade. In 1791 the potential of the place persuaded a syndicate to put up capital for development and Southend began to establish an identity separate from the old village of Prittlewell. Here a quote from Coller explains all:

"Of the olden history of Southend there is nought to tell. It is a growth of the last century. In a journal of 1768 we read;—'A scheme is on foot to render Southend a convenient place for bathing, the situation being esteemed the most agreeable and convenient for that purpose on the Essex coast.' Buildings were accordingly erected; but the plan and the projectors alike failed, and the matter slumbered till 1800. A member of the Heygate family then purchased by auction the buildings of the speculators, and patronised and improved the place. In 1804 Southend was visited by Queen Caroline and Princess Charlotte. This event stamped upon it aristocratic and fashionable character; and since then it has gone on extending."

So Archer's prophecy came true to the extent that the little south end of Prittlewell grew so large that it swallowed up its mother village and half a dozen more.

Priory Park, Southend.   *Owen Keen*

The Municipal Airport north of the town is a very busy place with scheduled services to Holland, Belgium, France and the Channel Islands. All the usual amenities are provided, including a public viewing enclosure, a terrace for waving goodbyes and a complete range of refreshment facilities.

139

The new Rochford District extends all the way from its borders west with Chelmsford and Basildon to the last tip of land on Foulness Island. It includes Rayleigh, once dignified as the centre of an Urban District which ran up the southern bank of the Crouch and included Rawreth. Rayleigh's popularity with commuters and retired people has led to a more than quadrupled population in the last fifty years, necessitating an almost continuous development into Southend and into Thundersley below Rayleigh Weir. The accent here therefore is on the provision of modern amenities rather than historical associations, yet there is much history in this place. For example, the Mount, owned by the National Trust since 1923, and always open, was crowned by a motte and bailey castle built in the eleventh century by Suen, son of Robert Fitzwimarc who, though Standard Bearer and Constable of England under Edward the Confessor, owned William of Normany as his liege lord, assisted him greatly at the time of the invasion and was rewarded with much land. So Suen's castle was surrounded by a great park which, although the castle was abandoned after some two hundred years, was still enjoyed by the Kings of England as a hunting preserve, for there is a record dated 1525 which includes directions from Henry VIII for improvements to be made there. King John visited Rayleigh in 1214 and subsequently granted this Barony to Hubert de Burgh, Justiciar of England who had great influence in the signing of Magna Carta in 1215 and set in hand the building of Hadleigh Castle. His career was halted by influential enemies who claimed he had used sorcery to gain royal favour, but he survived persecution to die at a good age in 1243. Incidentally it was his grant from Henry III in 1220 of fishing rights in Hadleigh Ray which is a documentary step in the record of the continuity of the Leigh fishing industry from its mention in the Domesday Book.

Rayleigh has now developed to the extent that a one-way traffic system has had to be introduced. This has affected the atmosphere of the broad High Street for the rush of traffic detracts from the enjoyment of the interesting buildings which gather in a particularly pleasant group at the top of the street by the church of the Holy Trinity to form a backwater in the flowing stream of vehicles. The church is largely of the sixteenth century with big windows making it light and airy. From the embattled south porch one can look straight down the High Street to the obelisk put up in 1908 to the memory of the two religious martyrs of Mary's reign who were burnt at the stake here. The men who built the porch would no doubt have known them personally. The landmark here is the old tower windmill which lost its sails years ago and was crowned incongruously with Tudor-style brick battlements when its grinding days were over. Now it houses exhibitions as part of a community centre complex.

Before leaving Rayleigh we should remember that it has a slight connection with that very interesting man Duffield William Coller who wrote *The People's History of Essex*, published in 1861. He was born in 1805 at Ingatestone and was intended originally for the Roman Catholic priesthood, but home circumstances changed and he left school early to be apprenticed to a local tailor. His feelings can well be imagined when he ran away from home and the tailor in 1821; but he was found, brought back home and then apprenticed to a shoemaker here in Rayleigh. This was once again more than an imaginative, literary fellow could stand, so off he went again, and with some success in contributing pieces to periodicals he kept himself until he could secure an apprenticeship with Meggy and Chalk, printers in Chelmsford. He climbed high in their esteem and ended up as editor of their *Chelmsford Chronicle* for twenty years or so before going over to edit the *Essex Weekly News*. He continued writing his own articles and was also editor of the *Essex Literary Journal*, much of which he wrote himself. He will always be remembered for his history of our county which first appeared in monthly parts. It is interesting to read what he has to say about Rayleigh, since he walked its streets so unhappily: "—now a second-rate country village with few mansions of much importance about it . . . We look around in vain for remnants of departed glory . . . Nothing has survived but this huge mound of earth . . . "

The B1013 and the railway run in a big semi-circle up from Rayleigh through Hockley and Hawkwell to Rochford. The railway station at Hockley has naturally attracted much residential development, but Hockley Woods, the vestiges of the great royal hunting park, have been preserved to the extent of 200 acres and are being administered carefully by the local authority with the provision of car park, cafe and children's playground at strategic points. North of the railway is Plumberrow Mount, a mound 76 feet in diameter, rising fourteen feet high. The experts are baffled by it. An excavation in 1914 revealed remains of both Roman and Saxon pottery but it did not help in dating the mound itself or explaining its purpose. The largely thirteenth century church away to the west is quite divorced from the new settlement. It has an unusual feature in its tower which starts as a massive square but above the buttresses turns octagonal, rising to a little spire above its battlements.

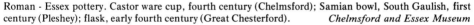

Roman - Essex pottery. Castor ware cup, fourth century (Chelmsford); Samian bowl, South Gaulish, first century (Pleshey); flask, early fourth century (Great Chesterford). *Chelmsford and Essex Museum*

Coller tells of how an enterprising villager discovered a medicinal spring near the common; London speculators seized upon the opportunity to build a pump room, for spas were then the rage, and Hockley was included in Dr Granville's *Spas of England* in 1842. "The proprietors called upon the afflicted to come and be cured, but they came not. The consequence is that the foundations of the villas have not yet been laid—the hotel which was to be filled with aristocratic guests is glad to catch a humble wayfarer or a village customer— and the pump-room, dingy and deserted, perplexes the passing stranger, as to the reason for planting this specimen of the modern classic in so sequestered a spot."

There is no doubt that Rochford, as an old market town, has been overshadowed by neighbouring giant Southend, for part of its airport intrudes into this parish, but it still keeps its market square, lined so attractively with buildings which reflect the changing tastes of time. The weekly market and annual fair were granted by royal charter to the Lord of the Manor, Sir Guy de Rochford, in 1247 and the last market was held in the square in 1959. The town centre is based on four roads named after the Cardinal points. The Rich almshouses, founded in West Street in 1567 are a reminder that Lord Rich died here in 1568 at Rochford Hall, although he was buried at Felsted. The Hall stands by the church west of the railway station. Anne Boleyn lived here with her family when Henry VIII was courting her with expensive presents and so it is quite likely that he walked the grounds which now feel the sprightly step of golfers, for what remains of the old hall is now the clubhouse of the Rochford Hundred Golf Club, founded in 1893. The building has been dated to 1545 but it has seen many alterations and some years of neglect before this happy solution for its use ensured its preservation for the foreseeable future.

The church of St Andrew benefits from the landscape of the links against which is seen to good effect the warm red brick tower with its projecting stair turret built in Tudor times at the expense of the seventh Earl of Ormonde. A church of another kind is remembered in the name of Chapel Cottages in North Street. On this site James Banyard first propounded his own brand of religion and gathered people of like mind about him. He was a shoemaker in the town who, having heard visiting preachers, was so impressed by their emphasis on the simplicity of true faith and worship that he determined to continue their missionary work in the town by forming a congregation and building a chapel. He preached to his Peculiar People, as his church was called, that salvation is the free gift of God. The belief which evolved in their creed, of healing through the laying on of hands and anointing with oil, was seen by the general public as a total rejection of medical aid; but the changing circumstances of our welfare state and its requirements in terms of forms and signatures has forced a compromise. The movement was confined to this corner of the county. A hundred years ago it would have been possible to see the People filling their chapels in a number of villages either side of the Crouch. They took their simple dinners with them in dishes and bowls, stood them on the big stove which heated the room, to warm up until they were required, and spent the day in prayer and praise.

Rochford can also claim a Lord Mayor of London as one of its sons. Sir John Shaa, a goldsmith, achieved that honour in 1501. The town's name derives from its position at the head of the river Roach; in fact it is a back-derivation for the river was un-named when the settlement was founded by a convenient ford which for some reason was called the "ford of the hunting dog". Later generations then named the river after the ford. History cloaks original meanings and leads to strange customs. Rochford kept one up for many years in its Lawless or Whispering Court. The tenants of one of the manors were required to assemble in the yard of a house at King's Hill at dawn and kneel in homage to the Lord of the Manor. The steward then very quietly summoned each man to answer to his behaviour since the last court in a whisper. Those who did not hear the steward's whispered summons were given heavy fines. Records were kept, not with pen and ink, but by scrawling with a lump of coal. The history behind this now long-forgotten custom is thought to be that it is a punishment for the rioting of the people on this manor at dawn on a day now lost in time.

From Rochford an arm of land runs north-east with the Roach on one side and the sea on the other. Across this peninsula stand three villages, Barling and Little and Great Wakering, the last two being united as a civil parish. They are both virtually cul-de-sac villages sufficiently far from Southend to maintain an agricultural environment. Their churches reflect their long existence. At Little Wakering St Mary's has a tower commissioned by Bishop Wakering of Norwich in the fifteenth century and, unusuallly, the rood stairs and their doorway have been preserved. Great Wakering lives up to its name in that it is now a good deal larger than its little brother. It is claimed to be the driest place in England with an annual rainfall average of well under twenty inches. The church of St Nicholas had an unusual two-storeyed porch built on to the Norman tower in the fifteenth century.

Beyond these villages the land is divided into islands by creeks which wind from the Roach to the Maplin Sands. Rushley, Potton, Havengore and New England are precursors to Foulness, and all of them reached by the only road there is from Great Wakering; built long and straight by the War Department which, since long before the last war, has owned everything on Foulness except the church, the rectory, the school and the hall. It is necessary to secure a pass to go down that road, something very rarely given, because the area is part of an artillery range and is put to other military uses, so little can be said about Foulness. At least the intermittent target practice is less offensive to the wild life of this isolated area than would be the development of a third airport for London and an associated sea terminal stretching out across the Maplin Sands as was proposed early in 1971. Essex people are glad that it was turned down, but it is still too early to hope that Foulness has permanently escaped.

Foulness and Wallasea Islands are washed on their northern shores by the Crouch and the first village encountered west of them is Paglesham, which divides into two hamlets, one by the church and the *Punch Bowl*, the other a mile across the fields at Eastend where the weather-boarded *Plough and Sail,* close by the Roach, offers refreshment to travellers. This was a place of suspicion and stealth when a good living was to be had from smuggling brandy and 'baccy in the eighteenth century, but it achieved also a good reputation for its oysters. To the west, still on the Roach, lies Great Stambridge which has its own Broomhills Dock close to Rochford, where coastal vessels can still come up on the tide to be unloaded. The tidal mill here, which was damaged by fire in 1965, can claim a life of five hundred years and shows that flour made the mill more necessary to the early settlement than the church itself, which here gives hints of Saxon foundation. There are two people connected with this tiny village who made a big impact, not just on England but upon the world.

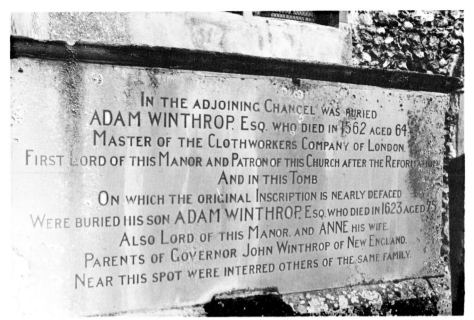

Winthrop tombstone at Groton, Suffolk.   *Russell Edwards*

John Winthrop, 1588-1649, lived here with his first wife Mary Forth, who inherited a fortune. She died in 1615 and Winthrop married three times more, fathering sixteen children. In the meantime he had emigrated to America and was elected first Governor of Massachusetts in 1631, to be constantly re-elected until he died.

John Harriott, born here in 1745, belonged to another age altogether, but had a life more adventurous than Winthrop's. As a very young man he was a midshipman who saw much of the world before his discharge while still a minor. He immediately joined the merchant service and then transferred his allegiance to the East India Company in whose service he was so badly injured that he had to be retired to England around 1781, but soon found another project worthy of his ingenuity. He bought Rushley Island for £40 and set about preventing its annual inundation by high tides. He had an embankment built all around it and so reclaimed a little corner of good Essex land. When the place had been farmed well and was making a profit, a fire destroyed house and barns. That was in 1790; the house was quickly rebuilt, and in February 1791 the highest tide ever remembered broke over Harriott's embankments and bankrupted him overnight. Such was his standing with his neighbours that they subscribed over a thousand pounds to his relief.

He must have been flattered, but the experience was too harrowing—he gave in and went off to seek his fortune in America, taking his family with him. But five years there found him no further forward so he returned to this country, still full of ideas; one of which was the formation of a body of men to police the Port of London where crime, particularly stealing, was rife. In 1798 the scheme he had worked out with Sir Patrick Colquhoun was given official blessing and, after trials, was adopted two years later. Harriott was made one of three special justices appointed to deal with cases brought by the new force. He died in 1817, a national figure of whom Great Stambridge and Essex can be proud.

Canewdon, north of Stambridge, has gained a reputation as a centre of witchcraft. One old village saying is that there will always be six witches in Canewdon, three in silk and three in cotton, one of them the parson's wife and another the butcher's wife. They maintained that when a witch died a stone fell out of the church wall and the witch was immediately replaced by another. Nobody seemed to care who replaced the stones, but I can report that the church is still standing, a splendid construction of the fourteenth and fifteenth centuries with a 75-feet-high tower. Said to have been built by Henry V as a thank-offering for his victory at Agincourt, it was also probably used in those early days as a lighthouse. At the end of the churchyard can be seen the village "cage" or lock-up and inside the stocks made in 1775 which would originally have stood on the village green. It is held that on this site Canute's men set their camp, a six-acre oblong with earthworks to defend it topping the rise of Beacon Hill ready for the battle of Assadune or Ashingdon, two miles to the west.

A Danish invasion force in 1016 under Canute was forced to retreat by the army of Edmund Ironside which held an advantageous position on Ashingdon Hill between the Danes and their longships, moored in the river off Ashingdon, and a battle was inevitable.

The *Saxon Chronicle* records that the Saxons were winning until one of their commanders turned the tide of battle by fleeing with his men, and giving Canute victory. Edmund Ironside was forced to share his kingdom with Canute and nominate him as his successor. Canute, it is said, rebuilt Ashingdon church in 1020 as a token of his victory, and the present church shows possible evidence of it. How our churches span the village story is shown here by another feature. The church clock put up to mark the coronation of Edward VII uses the letters of his name to mark the hours, with "E" at eleven and continuing DWARDUS VII REX.

Away over to the west Wickford, the Benfleets and Hadleigh occupy the space between Basildon and Southend. In 1887 in Durant's *Handbook for Essex*, Wickford was reported as "A compact village on low ground, encompassed by branches of the River Crouch, which is crossed by three bridges." But the ease of access it affords to Southend in one direction and London in the other has led to this description in the latest County Handbook, "Modern residential town between Shenfield and Southend and railway junction for the branch to Burnham-on-Crouch and Southminster. The oldest building is the small nineteenth century church. New indoor 'family' swimming pool."

Below Wickford, North Benfleet, actually now part of Basildon, spreads between the A127 and A13 while Thundersley and South Benfleet once joined in an urban district are still connected by residential development. Thundersley's name indicates its Saxon origin as "Thunor's clearing". The Saxons started chopping down the all-pervading forest and every generation since has done the same so that today there are more houses than trees. Boundaries have changed yet again and now Thundersley is the administrative centre of the new Castle Point District. From the hill on which St Peter's church stands there are some lovely views. Because of the rapid growth of population since the war the church had to be extended. This was cleverly effected by leaving the main body of the church as it was, with its thirteenth century nave and aisles and a fifteenth century roof sweeping steeply down to within nine feet of the ground. The eighty-year-old chancel was removed and, towards the east, a new extension was built on and consecrated by the Bishop of Chelmsford on 2nd April 1966.

There are still patches of woodland which can be enjoyed—Combe Wood, West Wood and Thundersley Glen, where good views of the Thames estuary can be enjoyed. South Benfleet is now so expanded as a dormitory suburb that it is hard to realise how recently it was still a little fishing village; but if we go back further in its history we find it mentioned in the *Anglo-Saxon Chronicle* as the place where Danish raiders under Haesten beached their ships and built a fortified encampment. King Alfred waited until Haesten himself had gone off on a plundering raid, sometime in 894, then moved in to rout the Danes. Records of 1564 show that five vessels were owned by the inhabitants of this riverside port which was largely used for fishing and for transporting timber from the woods around it. The church of St Mary shows its origin in Norman times, has a very nice porch with excellent timber work and tracery of the fifteenth century and interesting additions all through the years including the screen and west gallery designed in this century by Sir Charles Nicholson whose family actually lived here. The very names of the oldest inns, the *Anchor* and the *Hoy and Helmet*, show the connection with the sea and ships which Benfleet enjoyed in those Elizabethan days when they were built. The old beams and moulding still to be seen on their facades or in the bars were probably brought straight from the forest, which shrank under such exploitation, but there are still trees and open spaces.

Hadleigh Castle. *Owen Keen*

Between South Benfleet and Hadleigh there is a pleasant mixture of wood and downland on which the famous castle is situated—" . . . by far the most important later medieval castle in the county". (Pevsner) It is but a ruin today, and was even when Constable set up his canvas here to paint his famous view of the tallest remaining tower on the south-east side. It was Hubert de Burgh, Justiciar of England, who obtained a licence in 1231 to build the castle, but within a year, and with the walls only just rising, he was banished from favour. The King took the castle over, had it completed and appointed a governor, who through several reigns had to entertain royal hunting expeditions to the deep woods all around. In the middle of the fourteenth century Edward III saw the castle as a very useful deterrent to those impudent Frenchman who made daring raids up the Thames. For this purpose he virtually rebuilt it and these are the remains now to be seen. The castle and the land about it were settled as dower on many English queens down to three wives of Henry VIII. By then it was old and decrepit again. Lord Rich stepped in and bought it for £700 from Edward VI but, as far as can be discovered, he used it only as a kind of quarry from which the stone could be reclaimed for other building work he had in mind. Lord Rich's men did a thorough job and a landslide carried away the south wall and all that range of buildings in its entirety.

The view across the Thames to the Kentish hills is a beautiful backdrop to Canvey Island which because of its industrial development today and its residential expansion from earlier in this century cannot honestly be said to be part of that beauty. But that very industry, introduced first in 1930, has given a boost to the standard of life in the island, providing work and wages, contributing to the cost of local government and thereby assisting the improvement of amenities. It is concentrated on two industrial estates and is sufficiently varied to provide a good range of opportunities. No doubt Canvey is best known for its large oil refinery and storage tanks, but it also has a very unusual natural gas terminal in which the ice-cold liquid gas piped from ships is stored in excavated earthen "tanks" 130 feet deep, frozen solid by the very gas they hold and thus proof against seepage. The difficulty is that the intense cold creeps through the earth much further than had been realised and has caused problems with cracked roads in its vicinity. The four tanks hold 84,000 tons of liquid natural gas—just enough to keep Britain going for one day!

But Canvey has a history; when "Cana" came ashore and claimed it for his Saxon tribe it was standing a good twelve feet higher in the Thames—as was the whole of south-east England for that matter. His people would have seen Roman remains far more considerable than those which have been found recently in the "red hill" sites which indicate a primitive system of recovering salt from the sea practised even before the Romans came. As late as the seventeenth century maps show that Canvey, suffering constantly from flooding, was divided into several parts and no permanent settlement was possible until, in 1621, an enterprising group of local landowers, including Sir Henry Appleton of South Benfleet, commissioned Joaz Croppenburg, a London haberdasher, to build sea walls and drain the land. He brought over from Holland the great Dutch engineer Cornelius Vermuyden. Croppenburg was to pay the cost and to receive one third of the island for his pains. The project was a huge success; by 1623 the sea wall encircled the island. Many of the Dutchmen employed on the work chose to settle there permanently with their families and some of their names persist in the area. It must have been strange for them to see their countrymen under De Ruyter come up the Thames in 1667, having burnt Sheerness Dockyard, to land on Canvey to loot and burn.

A farmer from Canvey teased Daniel Defoe when he made his *Tour Through the Whole Island of Great Britain* (1724-7). He told Defoe that the men of Canvey could not find wives on the island, so they were forced to go to the mainland, to the "uplands" to find suitable partners. But bringing these rosy-cheeked maids back to the pestilence-ridden, fog-shrouded dampness of Canvey caused them to sicken and die so quickly, he said, that the men, used to the climate, were constantly having to bury their brides and climb the cliff again to woo another helpmate! Defoe took it all in good faith, it seems, for he wrote of the Canvey Islander who, while living with his twenty-fifth wife, had a thirty-five-year-old son who was already on his fourteenth!

The island continued through almost two hundred years as a small, rather isolated agricultural community. In 1897 it was half-submerged by stormy seas, but once again it was re-walled and re-cultivated and life went quietly on. Development dates from just before the First World War when one of the landowers sold off plots for house-building. The bridge built across to Benfleet in 1931 really speeded up settlement here. 1953 is a black date in Canvey's story. The terrible flood which swept the east coast broke through the island's defences and made life wretched for people marooned and left homeless: fifty-eight people died. The lesson was learned and the sea walls were once again rebuilt with all the modern equipment available and at a cost of over a million pounds. Those walls were raised to a height two feet above the level of that freak tide so that people can invest in businesses and in homes with perfect security. New bridges and roads have recently made travel to and from the island very easy. Now, with a population of some 27,000 and with all the services fully developed it has become a real town with all the amenities of a holiday resort—even a two-mile horse ride which runs through open country at the foot of the sea wall, the first of its kind to be set up in south-east Essex.

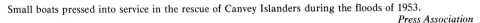

Small boats pressed into service in the rescue of Canvey Islanders during the floods of 1953.
Press Association

CHAPTER TWELVE

Closing the Circle—from Billericay to Dagenham

BILLERICAY has an unusual distinction. I know of no other place name which defeated the expert, P. H. Reaney in his compilation of *The Place-Names of Essex*. The origin of the name therefore goes unexplained, though its first recording has been traced back to 1291, which shows that Billericay is a very old town. The one great attraction to American visitors is the Chantry House and houses beside it. They form the shape of a hall-house built in 1510, but their fame is gained from the fact that the Pilgrim Fathers included in their number one Christopher Martin, miller, of Billericay. He was one of the three original men who in 1619 chartered the *Mayflower* and formed a company to emigrate to New England. He is said to have lived in this very house.

The Cater Museum at 74, High Street shows local antiquities, agricultural and craft tools, and makes a speciality of fire-brigade history from the Great Fire of London onwards, illustrated with models of fire engines. It was in Norsey Wood, which in part still exists on the east side of the town that the King's men crushed the defiant Essex rebels in the Peasants' Revolt of 1381. Five hundred corpses were counted in the wood that fateful night.

Thomas Wood, a miller in this place, had an enormous appetite and he turned the scales at twenty-five stone. It made him ill and he found the strength of mind to go on a rigid diet. He invented a kind of pudding, made largely of flour and milk, and ate nothing else at all for the rest of his life: he lived to the then ripe old age of sixty-three and received enquiries from all over the world.

The increase in industrial and residential estates around the town is evidence of the development of the whole of this area as the second New Town in Essex, called Basildon. On the way to its centre one passes through the Bursteads, Great and Little. The former was once of greater significance than Billericay, and, as the original settlement, contained the parish church, while Billericay's Tudor church was but a chapel-of-ease; and that is why both churches are dedicated to the same St Mary Magdalene.

The Essex Handbook of 1880 puts Basildon under Laindon and states it "is said formerly to have been a town." The tables are turned today; the greater area gets the old name and Laindon takes its place as just one district of Basildon New Town which had its first house completed in 1951. Now the town area boasts more than 31,000 new houses. Historial association with the earlier settlement is summed up by the New Town's own publication: "Basildon's most obvious links with the past are the half-dozen or so old churches within the New Town boundary or immediately beyond it. Several of these date—at least in parts—from the fourteenth century or earlier. One mile north-west of the Town Centre, St Nicholas, Laindon, crowns a wooded knoll; its black weather-boarded spire is a dominant landmark in that part of Basildon. All Saints, Vange, and St Michaels, Pitsea, command high points on the town's southern boundary, while Holy Cross is situated well within the New Town—its weathered stone contrasting sharply with the brick and concrete of the nearby Fryerns shopping centre."

The poverty of public services in this area, brought about by land speculation in the agricultural depression following the First World War reduced this part of Essex countryside to a rural slum, to an extent which could only be cured by action on a national scale. So Basildon New Town was really welcomed by the local authority and the County Council and anyone who knew the area in those days of plots at £5 a time and build your own shanty would admit the vast improvement.

The plan for the New Town provides for a town centre surrounded by ten "neighbourhoods", some based on the old villages and others, quite new, being given names which have always been associated with the vicinity. Each neighbourhood is virtually self-contained in all the services required, but the town centre itself offers comprehensive shopping facilities, a main library and the administrative centre, together with all the health, police, fire and other public services. About thirty public authorities have been continuously involved with the Basildon Development Corporation in this massive building programme.

Basildon borders on that area once called the Urban District of Thurrock and now known as just plain District of Thurrock in the new system of local government. One of the focal points is the new library and arts centre, though the one-way system means you can keep passing it in a car, but find it very difficult to stop at. Architecturally it is worth a visit, but more so for the sake of its good local history collection in the library, and the small museum which traces the history and development of the locality.

Some of the atmosphere of the old Thurrock, untouched by the growing influence of London can be seen from the foreshore, where an old lightship lies marooned, and the Thames runs on remorselessly. There is many an entry in the church registers of Grays of some unidentified body, thrown up on the foreshore, being given a decent burial. In the new Thurrock great efforts have been made to provide new housing estates and shopping centres in strategic positions, with the centre of the district focussed on Grays where a big, new shopping centre has been planned in the High Street. Other wonderful facilities for today's residents can be found in King George V Playing Field at Grays, where the Civic Hall and swimming pool allow for many recreations.

There are so many villages and settlements in this great district which have had a long and distinct history that it would not be possible to write of them all, so let us take some examples. Aveley has grown so that it merges into the London housing estate of Belhus, once the exclusive acres of Belhus Park, a grand mansion of which only one massive fireplace remains, now in Tilbury Museum. Here lived the Barretts who started off their Essex line with marriage to Alicia de Belhus in 1400. The family home was rebuilt in the early sixteenth century. Edward Barrett, 1581 to 1644, was one of the most distinguished members of the family, becoming Baron Barrett of Newburch, County Fife. He left Belhus to his cousin Richard Lennard on condition that he took the name of Barrett. So began a line of Barrett-Lennard which continues to this day.

Thomas Barrett-Lennard, who succeeded to the Dacre barony in 1755, was a contemporary and friend of Philip Morant, Dr Johnson and Horace Walpole. He had no legitimate children to succeed him, but a boy and girl fathered by him were brought up at Belhus in every manner as rightful heirs. The story goes that, on seeing his father's wife the little boy said, "Oh, what a pretty lady!" which brought the pleased reply, "Come to me, you dear little boy, and I will be a second mother to you." Of such stuff are novels made.

Moving east, South Ockendon boasts a church with an unusual thirteenth century tower in a circular form, built of flints. It houses a fine alabaster monument to Sir Richard Saltonstall, Lord Mayor of London, who died in 1601. His six sons and nine daughters are all represented. The side road past the church goes on to the Hall, a nineteenth century replacement of the house once surrounded by the moat which until recently contented itself with reflecting the image of the old mill. This mill was driven by water when it was built around 1830, but was later changed to the form of a smock windmill. It became derelict and was blown down in 1978.

The wreck of the lightship off the hard of the Thurrock Yacht Club.

East again over open country lies the village of Orsett, still delightfully isolated from urban development. There are so many features to be noticed in the church that in Pevsner's famous work on Essex buildings it occupies a whole page, and the timber-framed and gabled houses about it come in for favourable comment. Horndon-on-the-Hill is another separate village. It saw the long train of courtiers and servants pass by houses which still stand today, as Queen Elizabeth I visited Arden Hall on 5th August 1588, where she was entertained by Thomas, Lord Rich. The house there now is a Georgian rebuilding. It was from here, and from the associated villages of Corringham, Fobbing, Mucking and Stanford-le-Hope that the hard-pressed Essex folk began the rebellion in 1381 which became known as the Peasants' Revolt.

Below these places lie the Tilburys; East, West and just plain Tilbury where the docks are. The port of Tilbury was opened in 1886 but its continuing use is due to

On the landing stage at Tilbury.

recent modernization, including the installation of container handling facilities. Up to five freight liner trains can be handled here in the course of one day and seventy shipping lines are serviced by this port. Another great industry, giving employment to thousands and having national significance is that based on oil; its storage, refining, distribution and manufacture of by-products. Here can be seen the arrival and departure of giant tankers over six hundred feet long and transporting up to 28,000 tons at a time.

Until recent times the massive chimneys of the cement works with their banners of smoke marked, for every motorist, the environs of the Purfleet-Dartford tunnel. The cement works are there through an accident of geology. In this corner of the county, so handy for transport up and down the Thames, are chalk and clay, the constituents of cement. The larger flints that come up with the chalk are sold for use in pottery manufacture and the smaller ones meet the demands for hardcore, sandpaper and poultry grit. Well over one million tons of cement left the works every year. Since it had been going on for over sixty years, the vast areas of excavation all around the factory for chalk and clay have led to evidence of prehistoric life being turned up and this can be seen in the Museum.

Another, unusual industrial development is at East Tilbury where the Bata shoe factory has provided its own residential estate, including a hotel, restaurants, shops and a social and recreational centre. It all started in 1933 with one small factory and a few houses.

Thurrock has beautiful aspects in its little villages, and its useful and practical side in the great Thames-side industries. The Tilbury-Gravesend ferry took the shortest route it could, where the river suddenly narrows to just under half a mile in width, so blockhouses were sited on each bank, to prevent enemy ships gaining access to London.

If you make your way eastwards a quarter of a mile, past the *World's End* inn, you will be up to the outer defences of the fort upon the Essex bank. You enter it by the impressive old Water Gate, dating back to just before 1700, when the present fort replaced the blockhouse built in the reign of Henry VIII. The fort was substantially altered in the 1860's, but it still remains in its essential plan a very rare example in this country of the bastioned-system of defence in depth, which includes at Tilbury a double line of moats on the landward side.

When the first fort was built there in 1539 the garrison consisted of nine men, of whom the Captain, Francis Grant, was paid a whole shilling a day. Down the years it was alternately neglected and rebuilt, according to the national emergency. In 1724, Daniel Defoe, on his well-known tour, estimated that at Tilbury Fort there were up to 100 guns yet the fort was never required to fire a shot in wartime anger. The *Chelmsford Chronicle* of November 1776 records:

"Gravesend Oct 29. A terrible affair happened this day at Tilbury Fort. A great match of cricket being to be played between Kent and Essex, the parties assembled on both sides. When they were met, a man appearing among the former, who should not have been there, the Essex men refused playing, on which a very bloody battle ensued, and the Kentish men being likely to be worsted, one of them ran into the Guard-house and getting a gun from one of the invalids, (the fort then included a number of convalescent soldiers in its complement) fired and killed one of the opposite party.
On seeing this they all began running to the Guard-house, and there being but four soldiers there, they took away the guns and fell to it, doing a great deal of mischief. An old invalid was run thro' the body with a bayonet; and a serjeant who commands at the fort, in the absence of the officer, endeavouring with his four men

154

to quell them, was shot dead. At last the Essex men took to flight, and running over the drawbridge, made their escape. The Kentish men then made off in their boats, but search is making after them.''

A last look at Thurrock must focus on Chadwell, home of the Foe family in the fifteenth century. The celebrated Daniel Defoe started a tile manufactory here in 1694. He lived in fine style, but his urge to write got in the way of that business, which, being neglected, finally failed, and he lost a colossal £3,000 in the money of the day.

Defoe, however, claimed that it was his imprisonment over the publication of his book, *The shortest way with dissenters* which caused the abandonment of the business. He persisted in his religious principles and their propagation in pamphlets even while in prison, and also wrote a complete twice-weekly newspaper, the *Review*, which may well have been the model for the famous *Tatler* and *Spectator*. He was released from prison in 1704, and the stream of publications became a flood. *The Life and Strange Surprising Adventures of Robinson Crusoe, of York, Mariner*, must be his best known work, while history and travel books are pleased to quote often from his *A tour through Great Britain* published in 1726.

From Thurrock let us complete the circle of Essex by calling in at the new London Borough of Barking, which includes the old Essex places of Barking and Dagenham, with a long finger of land northward including Becontree Heath, Chadwell Heath and Marks Gate.

The old market place, Grays Thurrock.

It is almost impossible to visualise in modern Barking its original function through hundreds of years as a fishing port which developed from the fifteenth century to a climax in the middle of the nineteenth century. Then the Barking fishing fleet returning up the Thames was a grand sight. Two hundred or more fishing smacks, manned by some two thousand men and boys, coming in with the tide, and the quayside bubbling with excitement, waiting to know the extent of the catch and the dealers anxious to be the first into London with their stock.

All this was brought about by the humble River Roding which was navigable up to the old town and was known there as Barking Creek. Another curious reason for this continuing industry was the fact that in autumn the marshes could be flooded through sluice gates above the town. Winter's cold turned all those sheets of water into ice which was broken up and collected into the great ice-house specially built in the town. Thus the fish could be kept for export to London and its environs all the year round. The great name in this industry was Hewett. Scrymgeour Hewett settled in Barking in about 1764 and married the daughter of a local fisherman. Their son Samuel was the first to spot the advantage of this early refrigeration in fishing boats. He made it doubly advantageous by tying it to another innovation, that of keeping the fishing fleet on station over the shoals of fish while a fast cutter regularly rushed their catch to port. His Short Blue Fleet was highly organised and at its peak numbered two hundred and twenty smacks.

But steamboats and railways doomed this clever arrangement and in 1899 Barking ceased to exist as a fishing port. Much earlier in its story it had lost another valuable feature. Barking Abbey, built around 666 by Erkenwald, later Bishop of London, was one of the richest religious foundations in the country. Two hundred years later it was brought to ruin by the Danish marauders, but it was restored by King Edgar in 970, and William the Conqueror actually lived there while his own Tower of London was in the building. For hundreds of years it continued as a great religious and educational centre, a nunnery ruled by a series of noble abbesses from the great families of England. But it was dissolved on the orders of Henry VIII in 1539, and by 1541 it was quite demolished, and the stone used to build royal palaces at Greenwich and Deptford. Yet one small piece of that great building remained untouched and can be seen today.

It is the Fire Bell or Curfew Tower, built in 1370, late in the Abbey's history, and restored in 1460. Since the parish church of St Margaret's then had no tower the Abbess allowed the use of this tower as the belfry, and so its use in church worship saved it from the fate of the rest of the Abbey. An entry in the church marriage register records the wedding of the famous Captain Cook to Elizabeth Batts.

In the heart of the town, the National Trust is preserving Eastbury House, which under some splendid Tudor chimney stacks shows three storeys, the top one in attractive pointed gables, and all with characteristic mullioned windows. It is now leased by the Borough for social services, and for the moment the murals within, which show landscapes and seascapes, are boarded up. It was built by Clement Sysley who purchased the Manor of Eastbury in 1557 and was buried in the chancel of St Margaret's.

Dagenham today is associated in most people's minds with Ford's Motor Works. Since it is one of the largest car factories in the world, extending over six hundred acres and owning its own stretch of docks on the Thames, the association is justified. But there is an old village of Dagenham where the church of St Peter and St Paul still stands in a village street setting, a veritable oasis in a desert of development for industrial and traffic purposes. Across from it stands the *Cross Keys Inn*, a further symbol of the link with St Peter. It was built just about 1500, and so is the oldest secular building left in the whole Borough. Existing deeds for the place go back to 1670.

In the church a notable feature is the number of brasses, some of the latest in Essex, to the Urswyck family. Sir Thomas Urswyck, a judge who died in 1479, was of help to Edward IV, secretly admitting him into the City of London in 1471, after Warwick's rebellion. He was knighted and a year later appointed chief Baron of the Exchequer and built Marks Hall which was finally demolished in 1808.

The Civic Centre, at Becontree, is a stylish building designed by E. Barry Webber, opened in 1937 and substantially extended since then. The largest housing estate in the world at that time was built here between 1921 and 1935, out in original countryside, and it became a show place for visiting architects and town planners from England and overseas.

New estates have been built since the last war—one of them surrounds Valence House, which with Eastbury House, are the only two manor houses surviving in the whole Borough. It was put up about 1600 when the moat which you can now see on two sides only was probably excavated.

Some adaptation of the house had been necessary in the process of turning it into the old Dagenham Council offices, since when it has been used as the administrative offices of the library service, with a small, but growing museum.

One panelled room has been restored to its old state and furnished in the appropriate style, through the courtesy of the Victoria and Albert Museum. In 1963 forty-eight portraits of the Fanshawe family were presented to the Borough and are displayed here. This family has been associated with the area since 1557 when they purchased the manor of Jenkins in old Barking and the estate of Parsloes in 1619, which remained in the family for over two hundred and eighty-five years.

Down by the river Ford's frontage hides the evidence of a frightful episode in Dagenham's history. David Coller, in 1861 wrote:

"Near the embankment of the Thames is a broad pool of 44 acres, the standing mark of the inundation known as the Dagenham Breach, which in 1707 laid desolate this part of the parish. On the 17th December in that year, an extraordinary high tide blew up a small sluice made in the sea-wall for the purpose of drainage. This might easily have been stopped by prompt action, but it was neglected . . ."

The water tore open a channel 100 yards wide and 20 feet deep and a thousand acres of rich land were inundated. At the mouth of the breach a sandbank formed and, stretching a mile into the Thames, threatened navigation.

For seven years landowners attempted to seal the breach, but had not the men, the money or the resources. The growing sandbank was a real threat to shipping on the Thames and so Parliament levied a tax on vessels in the river to provide the cash. William Boswell undertook to do all the work required for £16,500, but after it was all expended he had to admit defeat. Captain Perry attempted the task in 1715, obtaining a guarantee from Parliament for the finance. It took five years, with heartbreaking setbacks from further abnormally high tides, to seal the gap finally, and the expenditure of another £40,000. The bank there is the Captain's memorial, and it ensures his name will always be remembered.

We end where we began, on the bank of England's greatest river, which marks the edge of Essex. I have been able to tell but a few chapters of the Essex story but if I have stirred a few hearts to pride in their county, and a few minds to further enquiry into its history, people and places I shall be well satisfied.

Tilbury Dock, the furthest down river of the P.L.A.'s enclosed docks, has the most modern equipment to handle container bulk grain, packaged forest products and r.o./r.o. traffic.

Photograph by Handford, courtesy P.L.A.

Bibliography

Addison, Sir William. *Essex Worthies: A Biographical Companion to the County*. Phillimore, 1973.

Booker, John. *Essex and the Industrial Revolution*. Essex County Council (Essex Record Office Publications No 66), 1974.

Brooks, C. A. and Smart, Alistair. *Constable and His Country*. Elek, 1976.

Christy, Miller. *Durrant's Handbook for Essex*. Edmund Durrant & Company, 1887.

Coller, D. W. *The People's History of Essex*. Meggy and Chalk, 1861.

Doubleday, H. A., Page, W., and Round, J. H., editors. *The Victoria History of the County of Essex*. 1903-1907. Powell, W. R., editor. 1956—in progress. 8 vols.

Edwards, A. C. *A History of Essex*. Phillimore, 4th edn, 1978.

Jarvis, Stan. *Essex*. Shire Publications, 1986.

Jarvis, Stan. *Victorian and Edwardian Essex from Old Photographs*. Batsford, 1974.

Jarvis, Stan and Harrison, Colin. *In Search of Essex: A Traveller's Companion to the County*. Essex Countryside, 1968.

Morant, Philip. *The History and Antiquities of the County of Essex*. 2 vols, 1763, 1768. Republished 1978, E.P. Publishing and Essex County Library.

Pevsner, Nikolaus. *The Buildings of England—Essex*. 2nd edn revised by Enid Radcliffe. Penguin, 1965.

Reaney, P. H. *The Place-Names of Essex*. English Place-Name Society, Volume XII, 1935. Reissued 1969.

Whitnall, F. G. (compiler). *The Essex Bed-side Book*. Essex Countryside, 1971.

Wright, T. *The History and Topography of the County of Essex*. 2 vols, 1836.

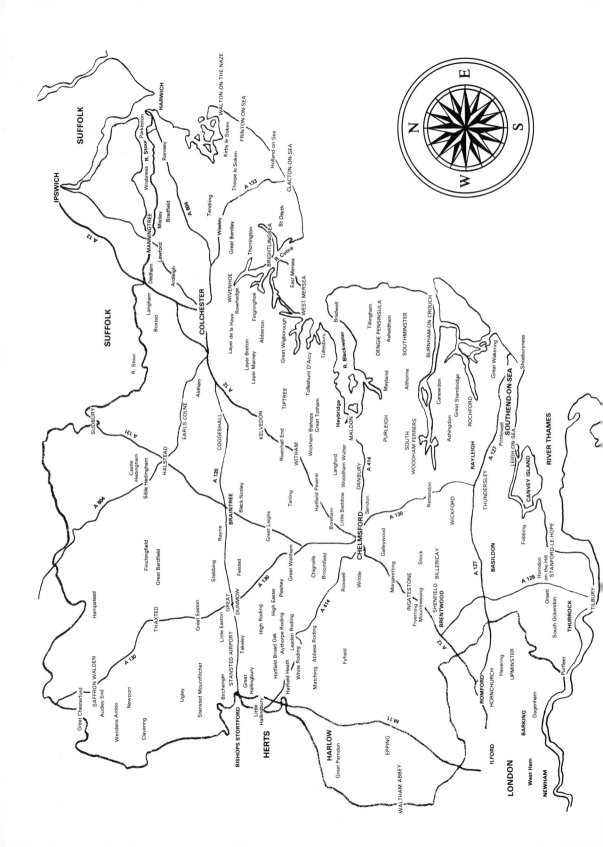

INDEX

INDEX

INDEX

Turpin, Dick, 111
Tusser, Thomas, 41-42
Twistington Higgins, Elizabeth, 27
Tyrell, Sir Thomas, 127

U
Udall, Nicholas, 45
Ugley, 103
Ulting, 2
University of Essex, 74
Upminster, 11
Upton, 9
Urswyck family, 157

V
Valence House, 157
Valentines Park, 10
Vermuyden, Cornelius, 147
Victoria, Queen, 109
Vincent, Clement, 85

W
Waldegrave family, 60
Walker, Kenneth, 67
Wallasea Island, 143
Wallbury Camp, 107
Waltham Abbey, 109
Waltham Forest, 1
Waltham Holy Cross, 109
Walthamstow, 3
Walton-on-the-Naze, 2, 3, 65
Waples Mill Farm, 123
Warwick, Frances, Countess of, 97, 113
Washington family, 128
Water supply, 55
Webb family, 57

Weeley, 67, 69
Wendens Ambo, 102
Wendon, 3, 4
Western family, 41-42
West Ham, 7, 8
West Mersea, 76
Whispering Court, 143
White Roding, 121-122, 123
Wickford, 145
Wickham Bishops, 88
Widford, 24
Wilkin, Arthur C., 89
William de Ou, 125
Willingale villages, 124-126
Wilson, Arthur, 47
Winckford Bridge, 118
Winstanley, Henry, 99
Winthrop, John, 144
Wiseman family, 125
Witches, 33, 60, 145
Witham, 36-38
Witherings, Thomas, 11
Wivenhoe, 74
Wollards Cottages, 29
Wood, Thomas, 149
Woodham Ferrers, 128
Woodham Walter, 85
Woodhill, 88
Woolley, Hannah, 103
Wrabness, 62
Wright, Rev. Philip, 126
Wright, Richard, 114
Writtle, 25-26

Y
Younge, Patrick, 28